Evolving Agricultural Policies and Markets

IMPLICATIONS FOR MULTILATERAL TRADE REFORM

This work is published under the responsibility of the Secretary-General of the OECD. The opinions expressed and arguments employed herein do not necessarily reflect the official views of OECD member countries.

This document and any map included herein are without prejudice to the status of or sovereignty over any territory, to the delimitation of international frontiers and boundaries and to the name of any territory, city or area.

Please cite this publication as:
OECD (2016), *Evolving Agricultural Policies and Markets: Implications for Multilateral Trade Reform*, OECD Publishing, Paris.
http://dx.doi.org/10.1787/9789264264991-en

ISBN 978-92-64-26498-4 (print)
ISBN 978-92-64-26499-1 (PDF)

The statistical data for Israel are supplied by and under the responsibility of the relevant Israeli authorities. The use of such data by the OECD is without prejudice to the status of the Golan Heights, East Jerusalem and Israeli settlements in the West Bank under the terms of international law.

Photo credits: Cover © 4X-image

Corrigenda to OECD publications may be found on line at: *www.oecd.org/about/publishing/corrigenda.htm*.

Foreword

Since 2001, when the latest round of agricultural trade negotiations formally begun, there have been significant developments in both agricultural markets and to the use agricultural policies worldwide. Shifts have been observed in the relative importance of production centres and in price paths for a number of agricultural commodities. Trading patterns have also been altered. At the same time, governments across the world have pursued a wide range of different policies. There have been changing levels and types of support provided to agriculture across different regions. Access to markets has also changed. All these influences suggest that the impacts on markets, economies and households of current agricultural policies are likely to have also changed and with it, the nature and source of the gains from less distorted agricultural markets.

This book explores a range of different changes that have occurred in agricultural markets and policies since 2000. It then assesses the impacts of current policies in light of these changes and provides an update on the possible benefits that can flow if further multilateral reforms to agricultural markets are achieved. In doing so, this book aims to inform and assist policy makers and negotiators as they seek to progress multilateral trade negotiations.

This book, and the research contained therein, was prepared by Jared Greenville, Dorothee Flaig and Hubertus Gay of the Trade and Agriculture Directorate of the OECD. In the preparation of the report, the authors are grateful for the comments received from Ken Ash, Carmel Cahill, Raphaël Beaujeu, Dalila Cervantes-Godoy, Emily Gray, Przemyslaw Kowalski, Andrzej Kwiecinski, James Messent, Frank van Tongeren and Trudy Witbreuk within the OECD Secretariat. Administrative and editorial support was provided by Anita Lari, Michèle Patterson, Graham Pilgrim and Janine Treves. The work also benefited from the input from delegations to the OECD's the Joint Working Party on Agriculture and Trade.

This document was declassified by the Joint Working Party on Agriculture and Trade in May 2016.

Table of contents

Tables

Figures

Boxes

Executive summary

Since the latest round of WTO negotiations began in 2001, world agricultural markets have evolved significantly. Production, prices and trade flows have been transformed while over the same period countries have also altered their agricultural trade and domestic support policies substantially. This study focuses on developments in world agricultural markets and in the policies (defined as domestic support policies and trade policies) of major agricultural producing regions that have occurred since 2000. World agricultural markets continue to face significant distortions from government interventions in the sector. While some of these are targeted towards correcting market failures, others are not and have the potential to distort incomes and welfare, reducing the potential benefits that are derived from the sector, the efficiency of global food production and the benefits from trade in its production (as a means of balancing food surplus and deficit regions at least cost to consumers).

The impacts of government policies on global production, trade and welfare (proxied by private household consumption) are assessed in this study along with the effects of possible multilateral trade reform scenarios. This study provides an update on past work through analysing the impacts of current policies and reform with reference to changes that have occurred in markets and policies since 2000. The assessments are made through an application of the OECD's computable general equilibrium model, METRO, in conjunction with the AGLINK-COSIMO outlook model. What is not modelled is the range of non-tariff and behind the border barriers that can also influence trading patterns and therefore production and prices. These remain an area for future research.

The results from this study show that the current suite of agricultural policies has a significant and negative effect on agro-food trade. Overall, trade in all agro-food commodities would be higher if current policies were removed. Policies limit both trade in intermediate products and in final consumption goods, suggesting that the development of global value chains (GVCs) in the agro-food sector, which have the potential to raise agricultural incomes and sector productivity, have been hampered by current policy arrangements.

A significant finding is that while many trade and domestic support policies are aimed at increasing food production, from a global perspective they do not. If policies were not in place, the level of global agricultural production would be virtually unchanged. In fact, when broadening the lens to also include food production, current policies appear to have a negative overall effect. What policies do is to alter both the relative mix of products grown and the location of production activities. Policies promote staple products such as rice and wheat at the expense of other production activities. Notably, the production of and trade in meat and dairy products are hindered by current policy settings. These products are also those for which future demand is projected to grow the strongest (in per capita terms), suggesting that the costs from these distortions if left unchanged will increase over time.

For agricultural products, current policies are likely to depress international prices, but the effects are relatively small. Further, for some products (such as wheat and oilseeds), prices may actually fall if the current suite of policies were removed.

Importantly, current policies negatively affect global welfare. This study finds that the negative effect on welfare, proxied by private household consumption, of current policies is more uniform across countries and regions than what has been found before. Both policy changes and changes in markets that have occurred since 2000 help explain these results. In particular, developed regions have reduced and changed the nature of their support; the European Union no longer makes use of export subsidies, and developing countries trade much more with other developing countries.

The impacts of current support policies have a number of implications for future multilateral agreements on agricultural trade and domestic support policy reform. First, they suggest that there is still something to be gained from all regions in pursuing lower tariffs and less distortive domestic support. Second, current policies particularly affect sectors for which demand and trade is projected to grow strongly into the future, for example dairy and meat, suggesting that the costs of these distortions are likely to increase over time. Third, noting differences across countries, from a *global* production perspective, policies are not promoting production, and indeed, looking at agricultural and food production together, could be reducing it. Fourth, for particular regions, the results suggest that calls for increased isolation or constraints on integration in regional or global markets are also likely to be counterproductive. Increased interdependency means such an approach imposes costs on both domestic markets and those of their trading partners, including developing countries. The rise of south-south trade means that an increasing part of the effects of agro-food policies on developing countries are from policies in other developing countries. Fifth, the world price effects of current policy measures are relatively small, suggesting that trade reform is likely to have fairly limited effects on some of the world's poorer populations. That said, prices in the absence of current policies would, in general, still be expected to rise and thus the food security and general welfare of these groups should remain a policy priority globally. But given the potential benefits from reform, it suggests that protection through tariffs and quotas is not the answer to problems of food insecurity. Instead, policies that promote productivity and flexibility in production systems; enable market engagement by producers (particularly small producers); and provide safety nets for vulnerable households provide better alternatives.

Removing all agro-food tariffs and all agricultural domestic support would be ambitious and is expected to be a gradual and iterative process at the World Trade Organization (WTO). That said, information on the current impacts of policies remains a critical input into trade policy debates and helps demonstrate that further efforts are still worthwhile. To explore possible trade reforms, this study also looked at reform scenarios that may be more achievable. These took two forms: first, agreement on some level of liberalisation (to varying levels) as based on a stylised representation of a modest level of commitments by all countries. Second, maintenance of the status quo but exploring this relative to potential "policy-drifts" that could occur.

The results from these scenarios suggest there are still unrealised gains, suggesting there are benefits in concluding multilateral negotiations. Overall, a modest reform scenario appears to offer only modest total gains both globally and to the countries involved. For developing countries, however, the benefits are more critically linked to the actions of other developing countries than those by developed countries. Indeed, the effects for developing countries from their own liberalisation and actions from other developing countries have a greater impact than do the effects of reforms in developed country. Critically, the results suggest that the development of global value chains in these countries could be significantly hampered by current policies. Despite the small welfare gains from modest reform efforts, simulations of possible policy drifts, based on trends that have already been observed, show that inaction can lead to losses. There is potentially more value in being able to lock-in the current set of policies than in reaching agreement on small decreases in protection. This is not to say that reforming agricultural protection arrangements should not be pursued, but rather that, instead of further delays, reaching a binding agreement that "locks in" current practices is of value. The recent WTO agreement reached in Nairobi in 2015 takes some steps in this direction, but more are needed.

The results of the policy drift scenarios also highlight that those most affected by increases in protection are the countries which impose such increases. For one country, modelling increases in protection in line with current practice also decreases total agricultural production. This has implications for policies targeted at achieving food security through self-sufficiency. The actions taken have been in the name of increasing self-sufficiency as a vehicle to deliver greater food security. However, as seen in the results, total agricultural production falls and so does income. These effects will work against the food security of households, in particular those in rural areas.

Chapter 1

Current agricultural policies: An overview of their impact and possible reforms

This chapter presents an overview of the main findings of the study. It first summarises the main changes that have occurred in agricultural markets and policies since 2000. Second, it provides an overview of the results of the assessment conducted to explore the impacts of current agricultural domestic support and trade policies on markets and countries and the implications these have for future multilateral reform efforts. Third, it explores the impacts of various reform efforts along with policy developments that see an increase in agricultural protectionism in some regions. The effects of these scenarios are explored for developed and developing economies.

1.1 Introduction

Since the latest round of WTO negotiations began in 2001, world agricultural markets have evolved significantly. Production, prices and trade flows have been transformed while over the same period countries have also altered their agricultural trade and domestic support policies substantially. This study focuses on developments in world agricultural markets and in the policies (defined as domestic support policies and trade policies) of major agricultural producing regions that have occurred since 2000. The impacts of these policies on global production, trade and welfare (proxied by private household consumption) are assessed along with the effects of possible multilateral trade reform scenarios. The assessments are made through an application of the OECD's computable general equilibrium model, METRO, in conjunction with the AGLINK-COSIMO model. What is not modelled is the range of non-tariff and behind the border barriers that can also influence trading patterns and therefore production and prices. These remain an area for future research.

A number of studies that have analysed the potential gains from agricultural liberalisation since the Doha round began. These studies have generally used models that have 1997, 2001 or 2004 as the base year on which the impacts are assessed. This study provides an update on this work through analysing the impacts of current policies and reform with reference to changes that have occurred in markets and policies since 2000. Further, it extends the analysis by making use of the OECD's METRO model that provides for a more detailed examination of trade flows better depict the greater interdependencies in trade that have been created with the increasing presence of global value chains (GVCs).

1.2 Important developments have taken place in markets and policies since 2000

Since 2000, global agricultural production has continued to increase and there have been shifts in the relative importance of regional production centres. There has been a rise in production in a number of developing regions, particular those of Asia and South America. Developed agricultural producing regions, on the other hand, have seen more modest to neutral growth, particularly when expressed in per capita terms.

Trade in agro-food products since 2000 has increased at a faster pace than in the previous decade (Figure 1.1). For agro-food products overall, trade has become less concentrated, with the share held by the top 20 importers and exporters declining by around five percentage points between 2000 and 2013. In terms of trading patterns, the rise of new production centres has increased trade between developing countries (so-called 'south-south' trade).

There has also been a significant shift in prices. The long term trend of declining prices came to an end in the early-2000s and was followed by a number of price spikes, most notably in 2007-08. These movements were driven by a confluence of mutually re-enforcing longer term structural changes in demand and supply, short term market shocks and, importantly, policy responses. Prices since then have generally remained at higher levels but are expected to decline gradually in real terms over the medium term on the back of sustained global productivity improvements. Further, while the price spikes during the 2000s also caused a surge in price volatility on world markets, post-2010, prices have been more stable and for most products have continued with what has been a long term decline in volatility. There are of course exceptions to this, with world maize prices exhibiting the opposite trend.

On the policy front, agricultural support policies in many countries have changed. Domestic support policies are more decoupled from production and begin to target environmental outputs; in some cases, support levels have also been reduced. However, in other countries support has risen. Overall, there has been a convergence in both the level and the nature of support between emerging and developed countries. Further, in many countries, policy interventions rely on production distorting support related to output and input prices rather than more decoupled payments or investments in the agricultural enabling environment.

Figure 1.1. Major changes in agro-food markets over the past two decades

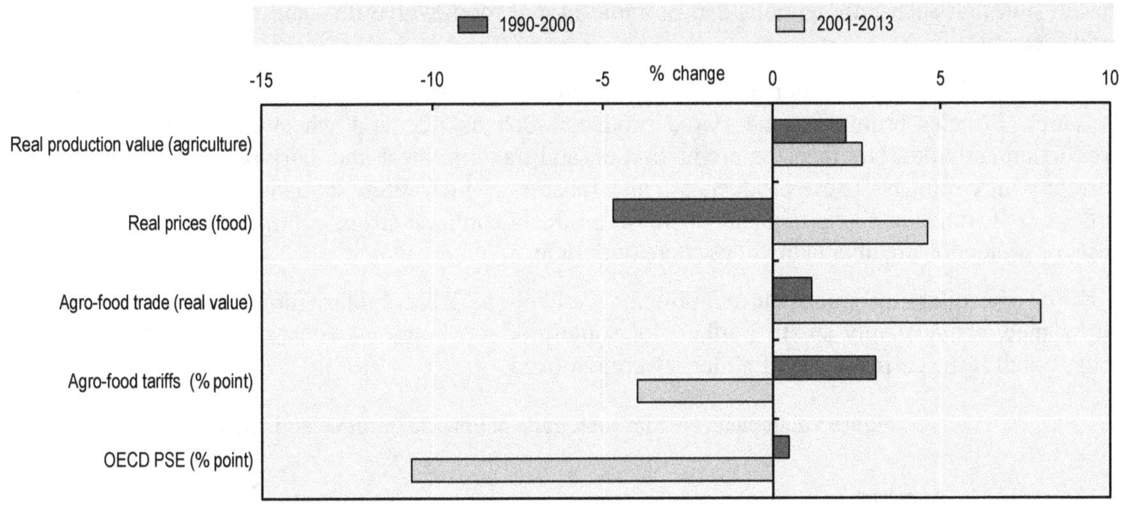

Sources: OECD estimates based on FAOSTAT (http://faostat3.fao.org/home/E)I OECD Stat (http://stats.oecd.org/); and WITS data (http://wits.worldbank.org/).

Agro-food tariffs have fallen globally, but on balance they still remain high. For many countries, tariffs form an important part of their agricultural policy settings; there are also pockets of very high tariffs. On the other side of the ledger, export subsidies have become less prevalent although new forms of interventions in export markets, such as export restrictions, have been more widely used.

1.3 Current policies continue to significantly distort markets

An assessment of the impacts of current policy settings as present around 2011-14 in this new policy and market environment shows that agricultural support and barriers to agricultural trade still create significant distortions to world markets (Figures 1.2 and 1.3). Further, there remains much to be gained from pursuing reform. Four scenarios were explored in this study: *Without current policies,* which represents the removal of all trade-related and domestic support to agriculture; *Widespread partial policy reform,* which represents the partial removal of trade-related and domestic support across all countries worldwide; *Uneven partial trade and domestic policy reform,* which sees partial removal of trade-related and domestic support in developed countries with very limited changes in others; and *Policy drift,* which sees some large emerging agricultural producers increase tariffs and domestic support while other countries maintain their current policies.

The current suite of agricultural policies significantly negatively affects global agro-food trade. Overall, trade in all agro-food commodities would be higher in the absence of current support measures. Policies particularly limit trade in intermediate agricultural products. In line with generally higher applied tariffs on more processed products, trade in final food products is also significantly affected. These two effects suggest that the development of global value chains in the agro-food sector have been hampered by current policy arrangements.

Policies also affect total global production and its location. A significant finding of this study is that while many trade and domestic support policies are aimed at increasing food production, from a global perspective they do not achieve this result. If current policies were not in place, the level of global production in agricultural products would be virtually unchanged. That is, support provided to agriculture in some countries does not increase production overall but rather displaces production from elsewhere in the world. Further, when broadening the lens to also include the production of food products, current policies are likely to be having a negative overall effect (driven by similar impacts to those seen for agriculture). These conclusions are important for international debates on agricultural policy reform as some arguments in favour of trade and domestic support policies are premised around the illusion that such interventions can promote *global* food availability and thus contribute to *global* food security.

What policies do is to alter both the relative mix of products grown and the location of production activities. Policies promote some staple products such as rice and wheat at the expense of other production activities. Notably, the production of, and trade in, meat and dairy products are hindered by current policy settings. These products are also those for which future demand is projected to grow the strongest. If trends in rising demand for these products continue (from continued income growth), the costs of protection are also likely to escalate over time.

For agricultural products, current policies are likely to depress international prices, but the effects, on balance, are relatively small. Further, for some products (such as wheat and oilseeds), prices may actually fall if the current suite of policies were removed.

Figure 1.2. Impacts on agro-food trade of policies, reforms and drifts

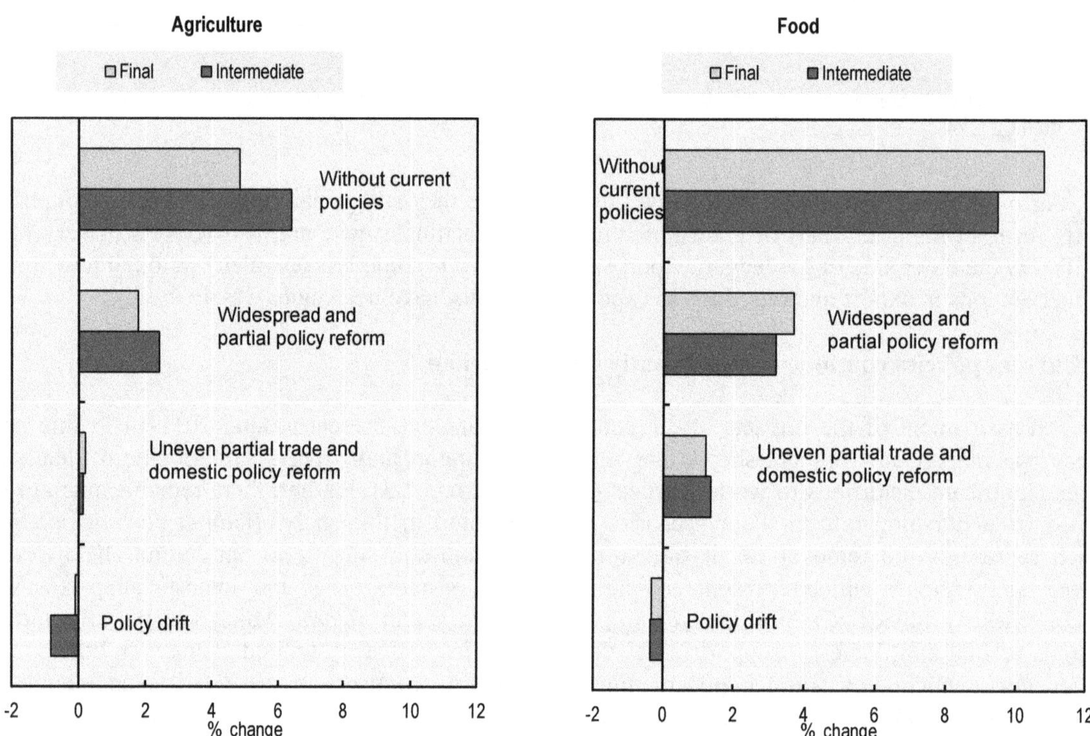

Note: Four scenarios were explored in this study: *Without current policies,* which represents the removal of all trade-related and domestic support to agriculture; *Widespread partial policy reform,* which represents the partial removal of trade-related and domestic support across all countries worldwide; *Uneven partial trade and domestic policy reform,* which sees partial removal of trade-related and domestic support in developed countries with very limited changes in others; and *Policy drift,* which sees some large emerging agricultural producers increase tariffs and domestic support while other countries maintain their current policies.

Source: Author estimates from METRO.

Current policies are likely to negatively affect global welfare. Proxied through private consumption, the negative effect on welfare of current policies is now more uniform and is seen across most countries and regions studied – a result that differs to findings by other studies in the past. Both the policy changes and the changes in markets that have occurred since 2000 help explain these results. In particular, developed regions have reduced and changed the nature of their support; the European Union no longer makes use of export subsidies (with the recent agreement reached at the WTO permanently eliminating these globally); and developing countries trade much more with other developing countries.

These changes have reduced some effects observed in the past where, due to reform, some countries lost benefits from lower food prices or faced costs from the loss of preferences (preference erosion). At the same time, the changes have increased the exposure of developing countries to policies in place in other developing countries.

This study also highlights that for households in a number of countries the benefits from reforms to agricultural policies are critically linked to additional government action. This especially applies for parts of the population that receive a high proportion of their income from agricultural activities. In some regions, the sharing of tax revenue or expenditure reductions gains for government from reform is necessary to ensure gains to households are realised, such as in India and the People's Republic of China. In others, households gain but governments suffer from falling revenues – such as in the Middle East and North African and Sub-Saharan African regions. Navigating these changes is important for policy makers and will also shape the political economy of reform.

1.4 Continued efforts for reform are needed

There is still much to be gained in concluding multilateral trade negotiations and reaching an agreement on partial reform of agricultural markets (Figures 1.2 and 1.3). Overall, modest reform scenarios – both unevenly applied focusing more on developed countries and those which are more widespread applying to all countries – are likely to offer modest total gains globally and to the countries involved. For all countries, the benefits from reform are created from a mix of their own actions and those in trading partners. Countries with high internal protections benefit from removing the restriction placed on their own markets, and if involved in trade, from the restrictions imposed by others. Given this, changes in world agro-food trading patterns have influenced the source of gains for some countries. For developing countries, in particular, the benefits on offer from reforms are now more critically linked to their own actions and the actions of other developing countries rather than actions by developed countries. Indeed, the effects for developing countries from their own liberalisation and actions from other developing countries have a greater impact than the effects of developed countries' reforms. Critically, the results suggest that trade in intermediate products between developing countries is most hampered by current policies and thereby the development of GVCs in these countries could be significantly hampered in the absence of reform.

Simulations of possible policy drifts, based on trends that have already been observed, show that inaction can lead to losses. Indeed, for some sectors there is potentially more value in being able to lock-in the current set of policies than in reaching agreement on small decreases to protection. This is not to say that reforming agricultural protection arrangements should not be pursued, but rather, instead of further delays in trying to negotiate modest levels of reform, reaching a binding agreement first that 'locks in' current trade policies and levels of support is of value. The agreement reached at the November 2015 WTO Ministerial takes some steps in this direction but more are needed.

Findings on the impacts of current support policies in this study have a number of implications for further multilateral agreement on agricultural trade and domestic support policy reform.

- First, they suggest that there is still much to be gained for all regions from pursuing further multilateral reforms.
- Second, current policies particularly affect industries for which demand and trade is projected to grow strongly into the future, suggesting that the costs of the status quo are likely to increase over time.
- Third, from a global production perspective, policies are not promoting production, and indeed, looking at agricultural and food production together, could be reducing it.
- Fourth, for particular regions, the results suggest that calls for increased isolation or constraints on integration in regional or global markets are likely to be counterproductive. Increased interdependency means such an approach imposes costs on both the domestic markets of countries applying such measures and on their trading partners, including developing countries.

- Fifth, the world price effects of current policy measures are relatively small, suggesting that there is strong potential for beneficial trade reform to have fairly limited effects on some of the world's poorer populations. That said, prices in the absence of current policies would, in general, still be expected to rise and thus the food security of these groups should remain a policy priority globally. The analysis suggests that protection through tariffs and quotas is not the answer to problems of food insecurity: policies that promote productivity and flexibility in production systems; enable market engagement by producers (particularly small producers); and provide safety nets for vulnerable households provide better alternatives.

The results of the policy drift scenarios also highlight that those most negatively affected by increases in protection are the countries which impose such protective increases. For some countries, the results indicate that increases in protection in line with current practice also decreases total agricultural production. The actions taken have been in the name of increasing self-sufficiency as a vehicle to deliver greater food security. However, as seen in the results, total agricultural production falls in time and so does income. These income effects along with the effects on domestic prices from interventions in agricultural markets will work against the food security of households, in particular those in rural areas who will have fewer income generating options and face higher food prices.

Figure 1.3. Impacts on the world economy of policies, reforms and drifts

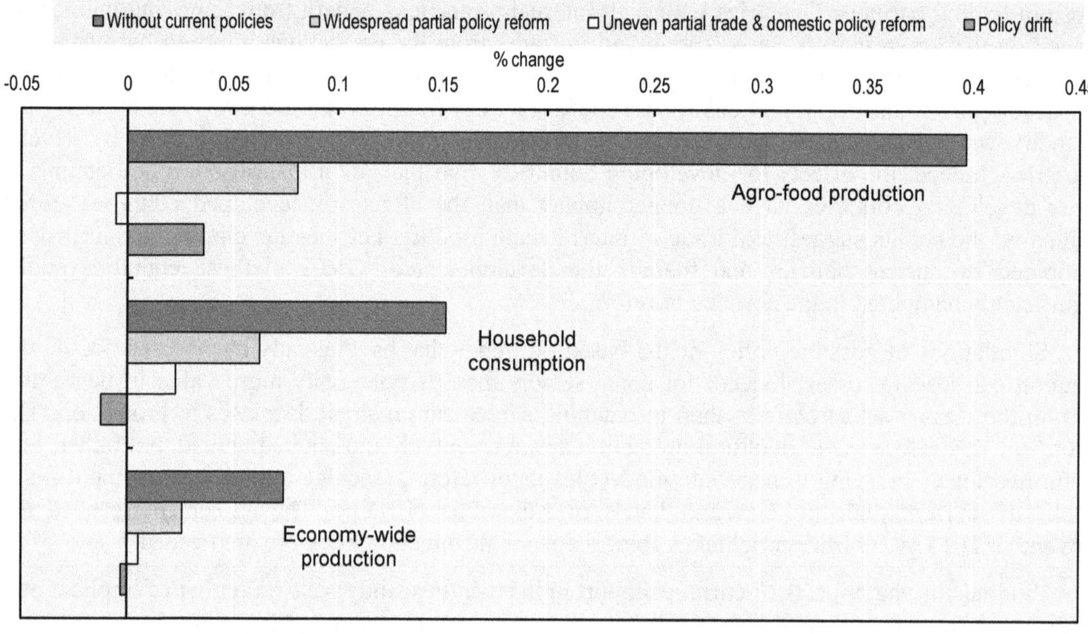

Source: Author estimates from METRO.

The impact of non-tariff and behind the border barriers has not been explored. These barriers range from quarantine and product safety requirements, to other requirements such as labelling. Some of those policies have also been increasingly the focus of regional and bilateral trading agreements. Exploring these barriers and possible reforms in the context of both multilateral and regional or bilateral agreements represents an area of future research. Similarly, the rural development, animal welfare and environmental performance of current policies have also not been examined.

References

FAO Stat. (2016), *FAOSTAT*, Food and Agriculture Organization of the United Nations Statistics Division, Rome, http://faostat3.fao.org/home/E.

OECD Stat (2016), *OECD Agriculture Statistics*, Organisation for Economic Co-operation and Development, Paris, http://stats.oecd.org/BrandedView.aspx?oecd_bv_id=agr-data-en&doi=83ff9179-en.

WITS (2016), *World Integrated Trade Solution*, The World Bank, Washington D.C. http://wits.worldbank.org/default.aspx.

Chapter 2

Developments in agricultural markets and policies

This chapter explores in detail the developments in agricultural markets and policies that have occurred since 2000. First, it provides a break down in the developments in markets in terms of changes in production, prices and trade. Second, it provides details on agricultural domestic and trade policy changes with respect to market access, domestic support and export competition.

The statistical data for Israel are supplied by and under the responsibility of the relevant Israeli authorities. The use of such data by the OECD is without prejudice to the status of the Golan Heights, East Jerusalem and Israeli settlements in the West Bank under the terms of international law

2.1 Introduction

World agricultural markets have changed significantly since the latest round of World Trade Organization (WTO) negotiations began in 2001. Production, prices and trade flows have been transformed, and along with these changes, countries have also altered their agricultural trade and domestic policy stances substantially.

This study provides updated information on the possible benefits of reform by exploring the state and impacts of current agricultural policies, 15 years on from the start of the current round of negotiations on world trading rules. It adds value to the current stock of research directed at the impacts of agricultural policies and trade reform by:

- Documenting the changes in domestic and world agro-food markets including changes in agro-food trade and domestic support policies, using updated information on world production, prices and economic activity.
- Estimating the impacts of current policies and differing policy reform scenarios with the OECD's METRO model (through analysis conducted with reference to a 2011 base year). The analysis provides a more nuanced picture of trade effects, as it allows for the effects of reform to be explored on different use markets (intermediate, household, government and capital). The analysis is complemented by simulations from the AGLINK-COSIMO model to gain a better picture of the price impacts of reform on key agricultural commodity markets.

The impacts of current policies: What is and what is not modelled

The computable general equilibrium (CGE) economic model used in this study makes use of policy information that is included in the Global Trade Analysis Project (GTAP) database. OECD estimates of domestic support to agriculture, derived from the Agricultural Policy Monitoring and Evaluation publication, are specifically included in the database. Data covers output subsidies, input subsidies (both valued added and intermediate) and payments to fixed factors such as land as calculated in the producer support estimates.

The GTAP database also contains detailed trade protection data, including both export subsidies and import restrictions. Within the database, the influence of quotas, tariff-rate quotas and other specific duties have been converted to ad valorem tariff equivalents. Data on export subsidies are obtained from country level notifications to the WTO and from the European Agricultural Guidance and Guarantee Fund.

The CGE model used in this study makes use of the GTAP 9 database. The base year for this release is 2011 where 11 new regions have been added with an existing 20 updated. The database also contains updated information on agricultural support, bilateral trade flows and bilateral tariffs (weighted average applied rates) and includes five separate labour skill categories.[1]

Similarly, the OECD-FAO AGLINK-COSIMO model contains policy information on trade barriers (tariffs and export subsidies) and more limited information on domestic support arrangements, again derived from the OECD producer support estimates.

Neither model includes information on a range of other policy measures that significantly influence trade. In particular, there is no information for the agricultural sector on non-tariff and behind the border barriers that could also have a significant impact on trade. These range from quarantine and product safety requirements, to other requirements such as labelling and barriers to trade created by differences in regulatory approaches (Box 2.1). Similarly, policies related to ad-hoc export restrictions and food aid, state-trading and the effects of changes in price volatility are not explicitly modelled. As such, the impacts, and possible gains from the reform, of these policies are not part of the analysis conducted in this study. These effects could both under- and over-state the possible changes observed with the removal of the policies analysed depending on whether it is the modelled barrier or not that has constrained trade and the extent to which any non-tariff and behind the border barriers are already captured in the level of trade flows and supply elasticities.[2] Many of these will partially be captured in the characteristics of the underlying database and as such, the results implicitly assume that these factors remain unchanged. Therefore, for a number of these measures, reforms would be expected to yield additional impacts to those presented in this study (see, for example, Winchester, 2009).

Box 2.1. Other notable influences on agro-food trade

Barriers to the flow of agro-food goods from one region to another, brought about by government intervention apart from direct taxation or quantity limits on imports, have generally been termed non-tariff and behind the border barriers. These groups include a wide range of policy measures employed by governments. Non-tariff barriers generally refer to barriers that exist for products and services moving across borders unrelated to taxes and quotas. They include measures such as Sanitary and Phyto-Sanitary (SPS) and Technical Barriers to Trade (TBT). Many of these provisions are imposed to achieve environmental objectives and to ensure domestic production systems remain disease or pest free. Behind the border barriers generally refer to characteristics of the domestic regulatory environment that create difficulties or costs for international suppliers. They include domestic interventions to protect consumers such as food labelling, handling, safety, traceability and other such measures along with licensing and other requirements placed on suppliers. Behind the border barriers can simply be created by differences in regulatory regimes between two countries.

The extent to which behind the border, SPS and TBT measures distort efficient trade depends on their design, the underlying market failures which they address, the extent of coordination across countries and, importantly, their implementation and enforcement. Unpacking these effects is difficult and contentious. What has been highlighted is that in aggregate, such measures do impact trade flows (justifiably or not). Disdier et al. (2008), for example, estimate that the effect of SPS and TBT arrangements on the whole is to negatively influence trade flows. This effect was more pronounced for trade between OECD and non-OECD members than between OECD members. Despite this, comparisons between different sectors indicate that SPS and TBT arrangements may also foster trade – highlighting the difficultly in attempting to determine the distortions potentially created by such measures. In a similar vein, Winchester (2009) suggests that reforms to trading arrangements that only focus on tariff and other border measures will produce much smaller gains than if non-tariff barriers are included. For New Zealand, Winchester (2009) finds that welfare gains from agro-food trade reform including the elimination of non-tariff barriers was more than four times greater for a range of possible bilateral agreements than if only tariff barriers were removed.

Making use of a meta-analysis of a range of econometric studies exploring the effects of non-tariff barriers, Li and Beghin (2012) also find that agro-food trade is most likely to be negatively affected by such barriers. Further, the effects of these measures imposed by developed countries are significantly greater on products sourced from developing countries, compared with those from other developed countries.

While not included here, it is worth noting that non-tariff barriers are increasingly becoming the focus of bilateral and regional trading agreements that are occurring beside the WTO multilateral system. For example, agreements that include such issues are the recently completed negotiations of the Trans Pacific Partnership Agreement (TPP) and the ongoing negotiations of the Transatlantic Trade and Investment Partnership (TTIP). The impact of such agreements on domestic agricultural production and agricultural trade would likely be a fruitful area of future research.

The two models used in this study are not explicitly linked. As such, the scenarios are conducted independently. Given differences in model theory, coverage and approach (for example, one is a general equilibrium model whereas the other is partial equilibrium), it is likely that inconsistencies between results will arise. In such instances, explanations for differences are provided. Despite differences, there are also a number of similarities in terms of the underlying data and economic theories that are used in the models. For example, trade flow data, border measures (tariffs and quotas) and domestic support measures are all obtained from the same underlying sources providing some level of consistency.

The focus of this study

This study focuses on developments in world agro-food markets and in the policies of major agricultural producing regions that have occurred since 2000. In Section 2, key developments in international markets are discussed, exploring changes in production, prices and trading patterns. In Section 3, changes in the policy landscape are explored, taking the three broad categories in the 1994 WTO Agreement on Agriculture as the organising framework – those of market access, domestic support and export competition. Policy responses as a result of the 2007/08 food price crisis are also discussed. In Section 4, the modelling scenarios used to assess the potential impacts of current policy measures, and possible gains from further agricultural liberalisation are set out. The results from these on the global economy, particular countries and for agricultural markets and prices are explored in Sections 5, 6 and 7. Policy implications are then discussed in Section 8.

2.2 Developments in agricultural markets

Since 2000, world markets for a number of agricultural commodities have been witness to a number of changes. In aggregate, levels of production across the globe have increased but at differing rates across regions; prices have changed in real terms; and trading patterns have altered, with world agro-food trade gradually becoming less concentrated.

Production

Balance of global production growth is shifting to emerging economies

During the 2000s, global agricultural production growth was strong, returning to growth rates seen in the past (Figure 2.1, top panel). Annual compound growth rates for the decade outperformed those seen during the 1990s, returning to past decadal growth rates of around 2.5% per annum. However, of particular note, the 2000s saw the fastest per capita agricultural production growth rates – close to twice those seen in previous decades. This means that during this period, agricultural production growth outstripped population growth at a faster pace than what has occurred over the previous 40 years.

Figure 2.1. Net agricultural production

Period compound annual growth rates in production quantities (%)

Decadal growth rates, world average

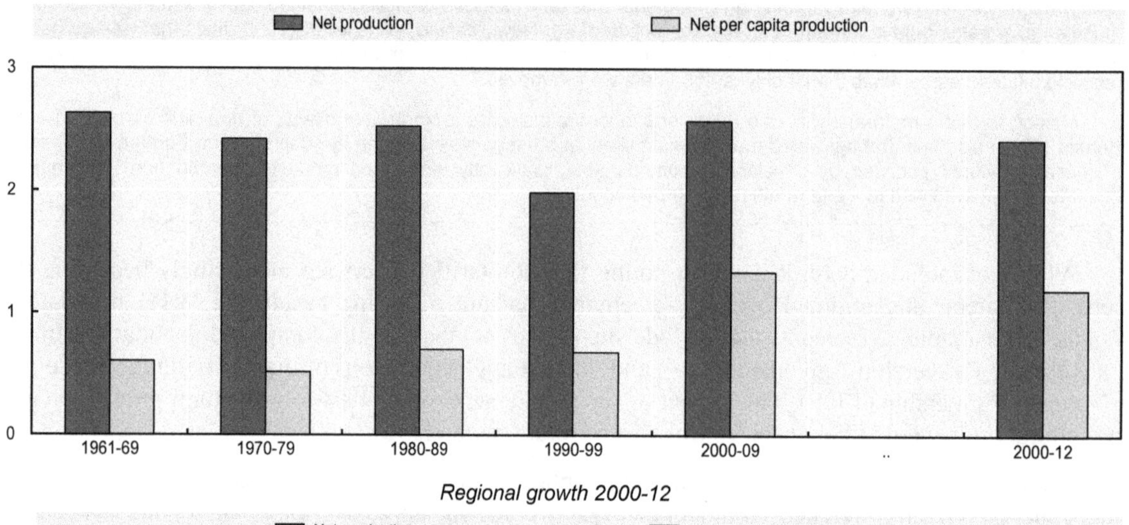

Regional growth 2000-12

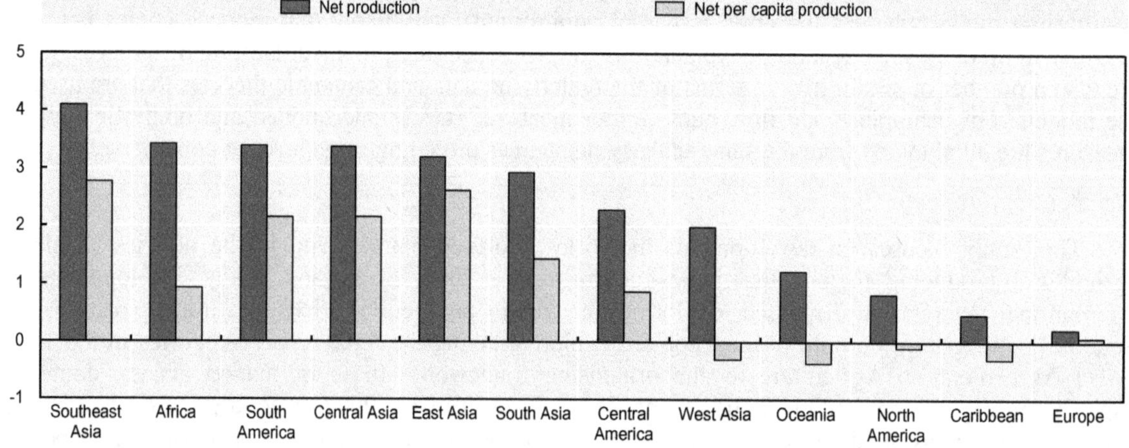

Notes: Net production refers to total production less cereal use for livestock feed. Growth rates are compound annual growth rates, that is, the annual rate of growth (r) in production (QP) required so that production increases from that observed in period t to that in period t+n: $1+r = \exp((\ln(QP_{t+n}) - \ln(QP_t))/n)$. It should be noted that if QP in period t+n is abnormally low, the estimated compound annual growth rate will also be biased downwards. This is the case for North America if compared with end year 2010, but the opposite for Oceania. Despite this, for both North America and Oceania, the choice of 2012 or 2010 continues to show growth rates below other regions except the Caribbean and Europe as per chart above.

Source: Author estimates based on FAOSTAT (http://faostat3.fao.org/home/E).

Growth in production was not uniform amongst agricultural producing regions across the globe (Figure 2.1, bottom panel). In particular, there are significant differences between developed agricultural producing regions and emerging production centres. The 2000s saw continued strong production growth in South America and Southeast Asia, continuing trends from the 1990s. Similarly, other regions in Asia (excluding Western Asia) also experienced strong growth. In per capita terms, both South America and Southeast Asia also saw an acceleration in agricultural production volumes in the 2000s compared with past decadal growth rates. For Africa, while overall production growth was strong, in per capita terms growth was significantly lower than in other developing regions due to higher population growth rates than those seen in other regions. Production growth in Europe and North America was significantly lower, and fell in per capita terms in North America, indicating the reduced importance of these regions to world agricultural output growth.

A shift in production towards animal protein

Over the longer term, there have also been changes in relative animal protein production levels globally and within regions. At a global level, the ratio of cereal to meat production (in value terms) has been gradually falling since the 1960s. The ratio of production values has close to halved over the period, and in 2013, the total value of world production of cereals was only 20% higher that of meat (Figure 2.2). Despite this, since 2000, this ratio has remained fairly constant.

Figure 2.2. Ratio of cereal to meat production

Ratio 1961 to 2013

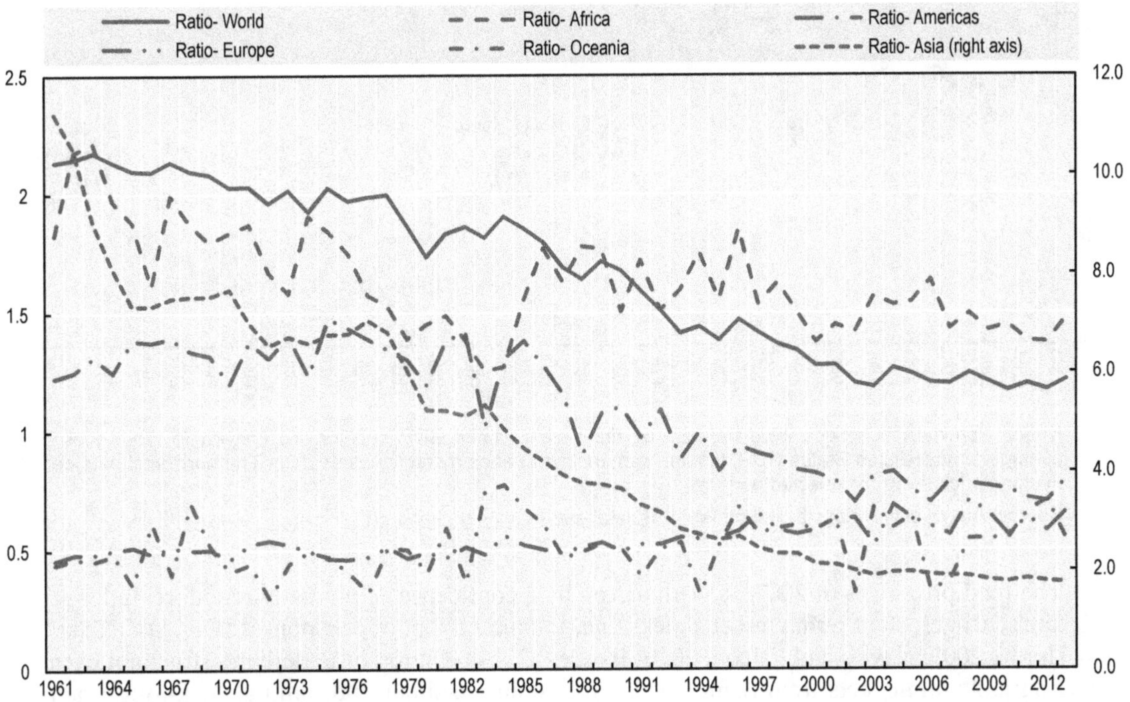

Ratio- World
Ratio- Africa
Ratio- Americas
Ratio- Europe
Ratio- Oceania
Ratio- Asia (right axis)

Notes: Meat production includes beef, sheepmeat, pork and poultry. Ratio is the ratio of gross production values in constant USD, 2004-06 base.

Source: Author estimates based on FAOSTAT (http://faostat3.fao.org/home/E).

At the regional level, both trends and the magnitude of effects vary. The most significant changes have occurred in Asia. During the 1970s, the value of cereal production in the region was close to seven times greater than that of meat production. By the mid-1980s, the ratio stood at four and by the early 2000s it was around two. Since, while the ratio of production values has continued to fall, it has done so at a slower pace. Declines in the relative value of cereals have also been seen in the Americas and to a much lower extent in Africa. In contrast, in Europe and Oceania, trends have gone the other way; with a gradual increase in the relative production of cereals compared with meat (Oceania numbers are volatile and heavily influenced by droughts in Australia).

Prices

Between 2000 and 2015, there was a shift in longer term price trends. Of particular note, the sustained period of structurally declining food prices came to an end in the mid-2000s, and was followed by a series of food price spikes from 2007/08 to 2012 (Figure 2.3). Since then, world food prices in aggregate have declined, but remain at higher levels than before 2007. Declines were particularly strong in 2015; however, these are conflated by an appreciating USD over the period.

Figure 2.3. Real food prices

Index (real) 1957 to 2015

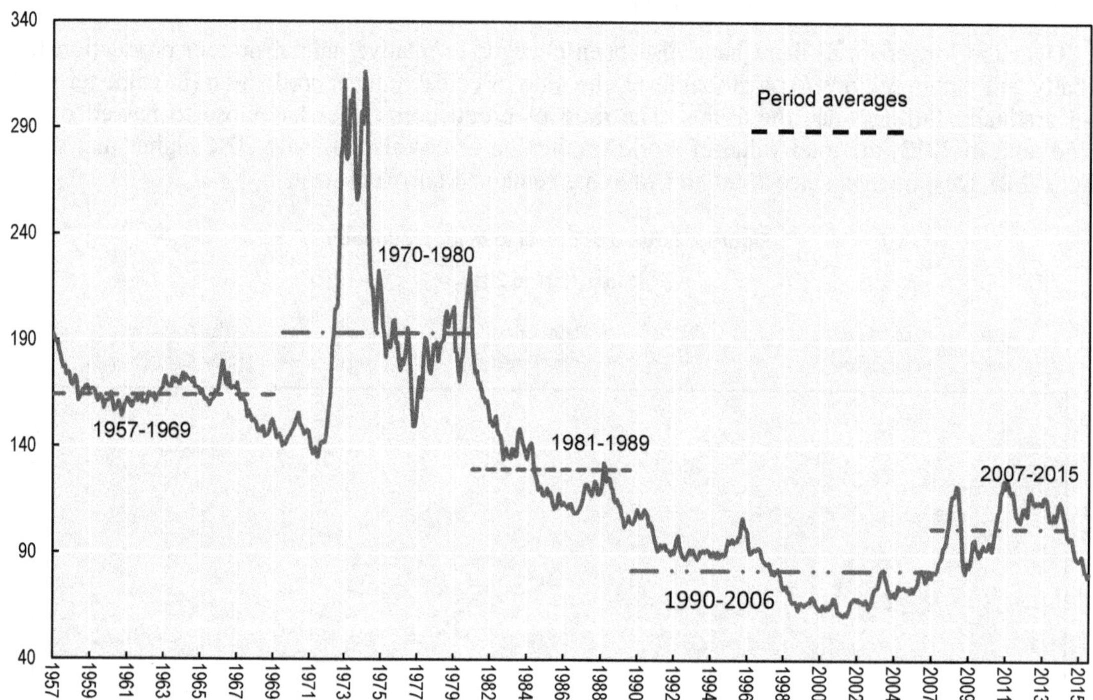

Notes: Nominal food prices were deflated by the United States GDP deflator. To convert to real prices, the average annual United States GDP deflator was applied to each monthly observation. The horizontal bars depict average price levels for selected periods.

Source: Author calculations based on IMF IFS database (http://data.imf.org/).

The food price rises of 2007/08 were driven by a confluence of mutually re-enforcing longer term structural changes, short term market shocks and, importantly, policy responses (OECD, 2008a; Piesse and Thirtle, 2009; Naylor and Falcon, 2010; Headey, 2011). On top of underlying structural changes to world agricultural markets from rising levels of food and feed demand, falling stock-to-use ratios and increasing production being channelled to biofuels production, world markets were hit by a number of short term shocks that placed further upward pressure on prices. Droughts in key grain producing regions and other weather effects, exchange rate movements, along with hoarding and panic buying by private agents helped spur already rising prices. On top of this, government policy interventions through trade restrictions and import measures, coupled with panic purchases by some governments, helped create the spike in prices. Government policies surrounding biofuels mandates and subsidies also contributed. Price rises were particularly witnessed for wheat, coarse grains, rice and oilseed crops – all of which experienced strong real price growth between 2005 and 2010 (Figure 2.4).

Figure 2.4. Real agricultural prices, 2000-15

Index 2010 = 100 (real) selected agricultural commodities

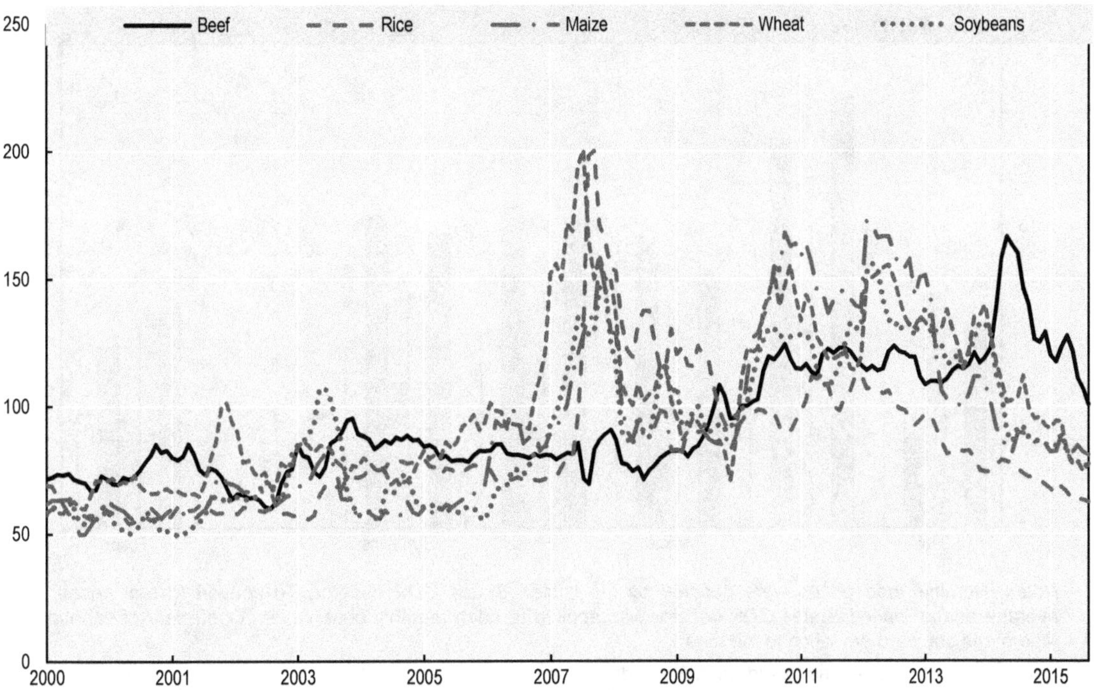

Notes: Nominal food prices were deflated by the United States GDP deflator. To convert to real prices, the average annual United States GDP deflator was applied to each monthly observation.

Source: Author calculations based on IMF IFS database (http://data.imf.org/).

Looking ahead, over the medium term real prices for most agricultural products are projected to decline (OECD-FAO, 2015). This decline is primarily driven by a continued increase in productivity that is outpacing increases in demand.[3] While falls are not expected to be as large as seen in the past trends, prices for cereals are expected to decline in real terms (falls for rice are expected to be the largest). Meat prices on the other hand are expected to only see modest real price declines over the projected period. Nevertheless, the projections suggest higher prices on average than those seen between 1990 and 2006.

Alongside the change in world food price trends, price volatility on international markets also increased for some products. Measured by coefficients of variation, price volatility between 2007 and 2015 increased for rice and wheat compared with the 1990 to 2006 period. However, price volatility for all commodities and food overall was much lower than what was experienced between 1970 and 1980.

Looking at decadal volatility, however, suggests that in most recent years (between 2010 and 2015), volatility for many crops (except maize) and food in aggregate has fallen (Figure 2.5). This continues past trends of declining volatility seen in international markets. This is not so for maize, in which the period between 2010 and 2015 has seen price volatility on par with that seen in the past. But it should be noted that the latest period is only partial, and over the full decade volatility may be quite different.

Figure 2.5. Real price volatility

Decadal coefficient of variation

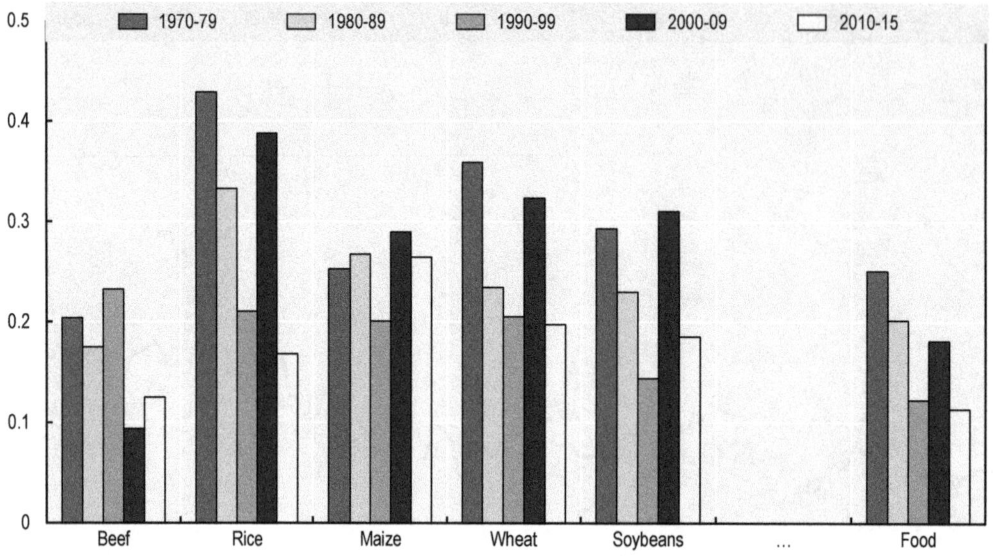

Notes: Nominal food prices were deflated by the United States GDP deflator. To convert to real prices, the average annual United States GDP deflator was applied to each monthly observation. Coefficient of variation is ratio of the standard deviation to the mean.

Source: Author calculations based on IMF IFS database (http://data.imf.org/).

Trade

Emergence of new agricultural exporters and importers

Over the longer term, the real value of agro-food products traded internationally has grown strongly. Since the mid-1990s, growth in agro-food trade has averaged around 5% per annum.[4] Since the start of the new round of WTO negotiations, growth rates in agro-food trade have been significantly higher than what was seen between 1994 and 2000 (Figure 2.6).

A major development in world agricultural markets since 2000 has been the increased importance of developing countries, in particular the emerging economies Brazil, the Russian Federation, India, Indonesia, the People's Republic of China (hereafter "China") and South Africa. Between 2000 and 2013, the emerging economies' share of world agricultural exports increased from 9.9% to 17.4%, while their share of world agricultural imports increased from 6.5% to 15.6%. Most of the increase in these countries' share of world agricultural exports represents increased trade with other emerging economies. For example, in 2013 Brazil exported around 24% of its total agricultural exports to China. The OECD-FAO Outlook (2015) suggests that these trends will continue over the next ten years. At a regional level, the Americas will strengthen their position as the dominant export region, both in value and volume terms, while Asia and Africa will increase their net imports in order to meet growing demand.

The changing patterns in world trade can also be seen through changes in the top 20 agro-food importers and exporters between 2000 and 2013 (Tables 2.1 and 2.2). While still high, the overall share of trade held by the top-20 countries also fell over this period by around 5 percentage points.

Figure 2.6. Growth in global agro-food trade

Compound annual growth rates in real values (USD)

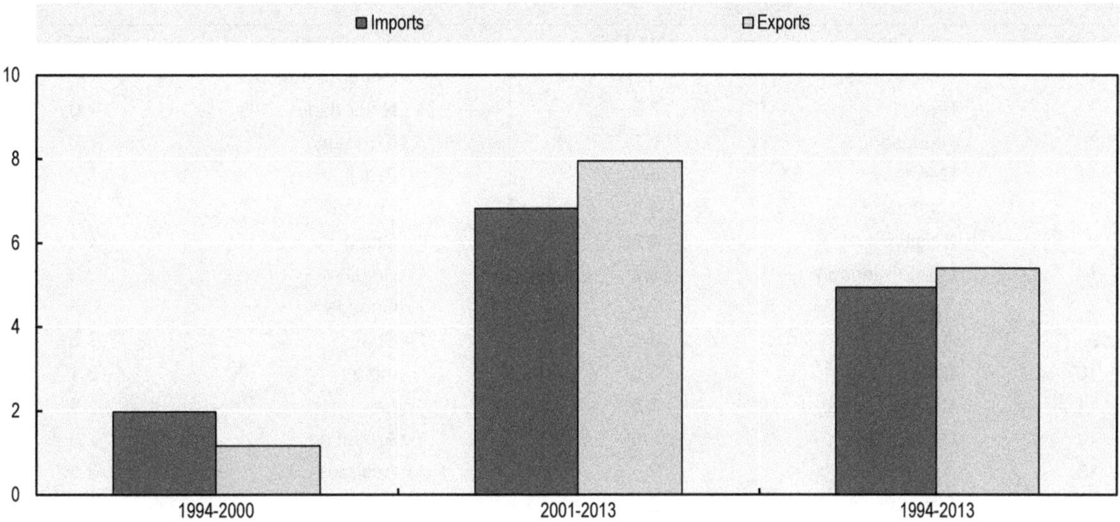

Notes: Trade values converted to real terms by applying the United States GDP deflator from IFS Online. Rates for exports and import differ due to differences and inconsistencies in country reporting.

Source: Author calculations based on WITS data (http://wits.worldbank.org/).

Table 2.1. Major agro-food importers

Share of total import value (nominal USD), 2000 and 2013

	2000		2013	
Rank	Country	Share (%)	Country	Share (%)
1	United States	11.7	United States	9.1
2	Japan	10.8	China	8.1
3	Germany	7.6	Germany	6.9
4	United Kingdom	6.5	Japan	5.2
5	France	5.4	United Kingdom	4.7
6	Italy	5.0	Netherlands	4.7
7	Netherlands	3.9	France	4.3
8	Belgium	3.4	Italy	3.7
9	Spain	3.1	Belgium	3.1
10	Canada	2.7	Russian Federation	3.0
11	China	2.4	Spain	2.6
12	Hong Kong, China	2.2	Canada	2.5
13	Mexico	2.1	Korea	1.9
14	Korea	2.0	Mexico	1.9
15	Russian Federation	1.6	Hong Kong, China	1.9
16	Denmark	1.2	Saudi Arabia	1.6
17	Saudi Arabia	1.1	Poland	1.3
18	Switzerland	1.1	Indonesia	1.3
19	Portugal	1.0	India	1.3
20	Sweden	1.0	Sweden	1.2
Total		**75.5**		**70.3**

Source: Author calculations based on WITS data (http://wits.worldbank.org/).

Table 2.2. Major agro-food exporters

Share by total export value (nominal USD), 2000 and 2013

	2000		2013	
Rank	Country	Share (%)	Country	Share (%)
1	United States	13.1	United States	10.1
2	France	7.8	Netherlands	7.0
3	Netherlands	7.3	Germany	6.0
4	Germany	5.5	Brazil	5.7
5	Canada	4.1	France	5.3
6	Belgium	4.0	China	4.4
7	United Kingdom	3.7	Belgium	3.3
8	Spain	3.6	Canada	3.3
9	Australia	3.5	Spain	3.3
10	Italy	3.5	India	3.1
11	China	3.5	Italy	2.9
12	Brazil	2.9	Argentina	2.8
13	Argentina	2.6	Australia	2.5
14	Denmark	2.4	Indonesia	2.2
15	Thailand	2.3	United Kingdom	2.1
16	Mexico	1.8	Thailand	2.1
17	New Zealand	1.6	Poland	1.8
18	Ireland	1.5	Malaysia	1.7
19	India	1.3	New Zealand	1.6
20	Indonesia	1.3	Mexico	1.6
Total		**77.3**		**72.7**

Source: Author calculations based on WITS data (http://wits.worldbank.org/).

In both 2000 and 2013, the United States is the largest agro-food trader, accounting for around 10% of both imports and exports. However, the increasing role in world trade played by China, Brazil, India and Indonesia can be seen. In particular for imports, China's share of total agro-food imports rose from 2.4% to 8.1% over the period.

More generally, the importance for low and middle income countries of markets in other low to middle income countries for their own products, and sources of supply, has increased since 2000. In terms of imports, since 2000 the share of total agro-food imports in low and middle income countries sourced from other low and middle income has increased from around 45% to around to 57% in 2013 (Figure 2.7). Similarly, agro-food exports from low and middle income countries to other low and middle income countries have risen from 35% in 2000 to 55% in 2013. This increased 'south-south' trade suggests that trade and domestic support policies in developing countries are most likely to affect other developing countries.

Falling concentration in world trade

Not only has there been a change in the relative importance of a number of the major agro-food exporters and importers, so too has there been a change in the distribution of trade between countries. As seen in Tables 2.1 and 2.2, trade in agro-food products is very concentrated, but it is becoming gradually less so over time. Using the Gini coefficient to measure the concentration of trade[5] shows that while the period between 1996 and 2000 saw a further concentration in agro-food trade (both imports and exports), since then this concentration has begun to fall, most notably since 2007 (Figure 2.8). In part, this is because of the emergence of both new suppliers and new markets for products over time.

Figure 2.7. Increasing importance of 'South-South' trade

Relative to year 2000 shares (Index 2000 = 100)

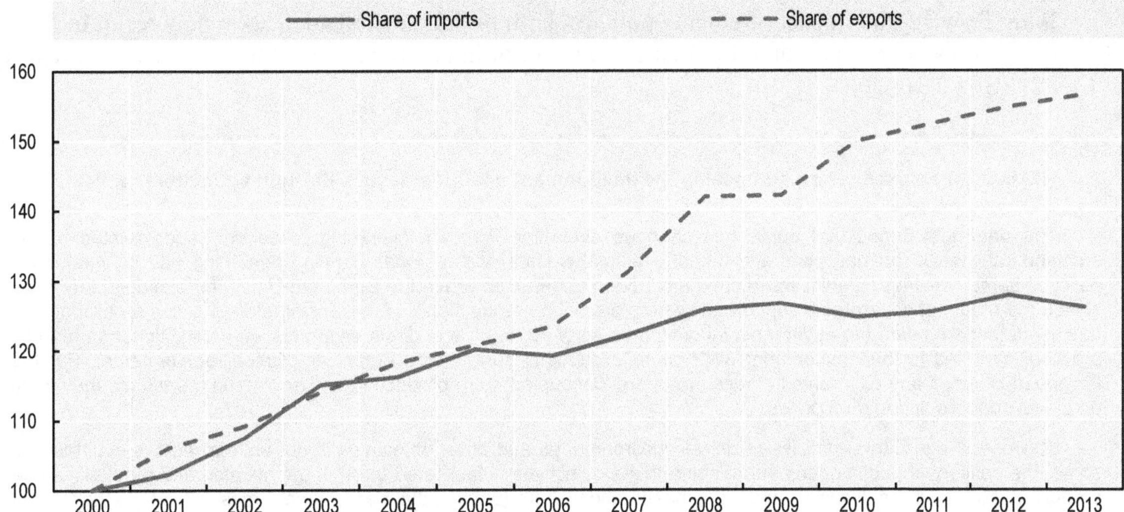

Note: 'South' countries defined as those within the WTO groupings of low and middle income countries and non-WTO members.

Source: Author calculations based on WITS data (http://wits.worldbank.org/).

Figure 2.8. Concentration of world agro-food trade, 1996-2013

Gini coefficient

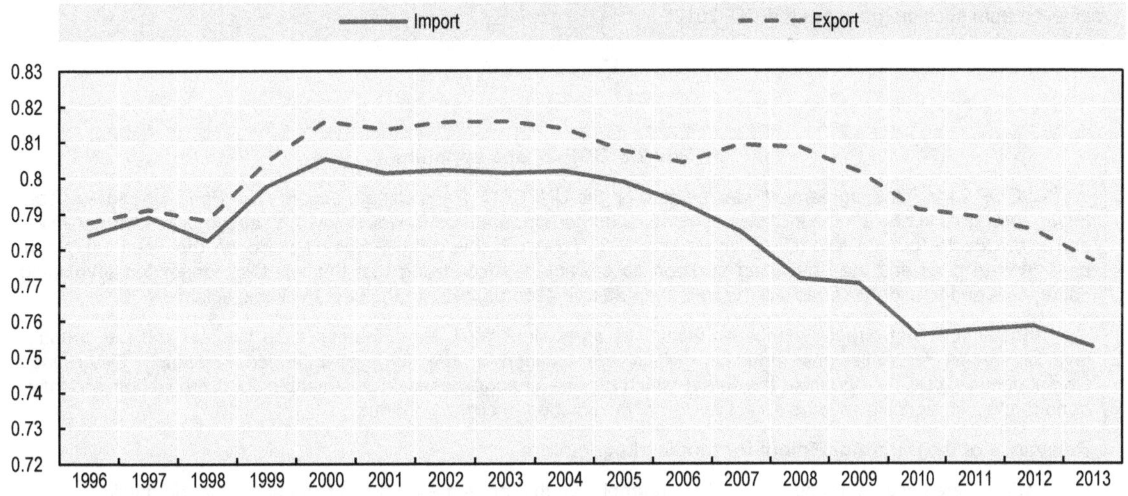

Import

Export

Note: Gini coefficient is used as a measure of concentration in trade.

Source: Author calculations based on WITS data (http://wits.worldbank.org/).

2.3 Developments in agricultural policies

The agricultural policy landscape has changed significantly since 2000. A number of forces have shaped policy developments, including changing market dynamics, experiences of past reforms prompting unilateral actions, a rising number of regional and bilateral trade agreements and importantly, food price spikes and the resulting food crisis of 2007/08. For some countries, there have also been broader changes to the objectives of government support provided to agriculture. In particular, there has been a rising importance of objectives and policies related to the environment, health and animal welfare. The methods used to achieve these objectives have differed across different countries given different perspectives on the role of agricultural policy in this space (Box 2.2). In sum, the range of changes has resulted in changes in market access, domestic support and export competition.

Going forward, the impact of climate policies, both mitigation and adaptation may result in further changes to the nature of agricultural policies as a result of international agreements such as that reached at COP21 (Box 2.3).

Box 2.2. Perspectives on addressing the environment and other issues through agricultural policy

The nature of agricultural policy has changed over time with an increasing focus on issues related to the environment, health (animal, plant and human), animal welfare and regional planning becoming part of agricultural policy in some countries. Significant reforms have been undertaken within the European Union, for example, that have shifted the nature of government support away from promoting production and influencing market prices for products to payments that are related to environmental outcomes. In of 2015, 35% of direct payments were conditional on farming practices targeted to the environment (with some exceptions surrounding cross-compliance requirements). For the European Union, many payments in these areas are 'decoupled' from production and so vary in the effects they have on global supplies and market prices.

The use of agricultural policies to deliver environmental and other objectives is not uniform across countries. In some, the delivery of public goods surrounding these objectives is facilitated through the taxation and regulations that prohibit certain practices. Policies supporting health and welfare (animal, plant and human) most often take the form of regulatory instruments that seek to constraint certain behaviours and practices and encourage others.

More fundamental, there is a debate surrounding whether agricultural production co-producers environmental and other public goods. Discussions on the multifunctionality of agriculture – the notion that agriculture not only provides food and fibre by also non-commodity outputs – have revealed varying views on the role of government and agricultural policy in this area. These varying views are also replicated in varying policy approaches across countries.

The effects of using agricultural policy instruments, either coupled with, or decoupled from, production on both achieving environmental outcomes or on markets are unclear (OECD, 2008b). While progress has been made to better measure the effects, significant uncertainties remain as there are significant difficulties in measuring the outputs achieved from such programmes (OECD, 2012).

Box 2.3. COP-21 and agriculture

At COP 21 in Paris, agreement was reached on the UNFCCC[1] Paris climate accord. The Paris Agreement[1] sets a long-term goal to contain the increase in global average temperatures to well below 2°C above pre-industrial levels and a pledge to "pursue efforts" to limit it to 1.5°C. To reach this goal, Parties agreed on the need for global emissions to peak and start declining as soon as possible – recognising that this will take longer for developing countries – and to undertake rapid reductions thereafter in accordance with the best available science.

Agriculture is not directly mentioned within the agreement itself. Nevertheless, both the text and the country-level strategies for emissions reduction, which are outlined in the form of Intended Nationally Determined Contributions (INDCs), recognise the threat which climate change poses to sustainable food production and offer opportunities for agriculture to be an active part of the solution to climate change.

Relevance of the Paris Agreement for food and agriculture

Explicit reference is made within the preamble of the agreement to food security and production, which acknowledges "the fundamental priority of safeguarding food security and ending hunger, and the particular vulnerabilities of food production systems to the adverse impacts of climate change". Moreover, Article 2 of the agreement underlines the importance of food production, clearly stating that "This agreement (...) aims to strengthen the global response to climate change (...) in a manner that does not threaten food production".

By giving governments the freedom to decide exactly which emission sources to address, the agreement does not rule out mitigation in agriculture. Article 4.1, for example, states governments' aim to "*achieve a balance between anthropogenic emissions by sources and removals by sinks of* greenhouse *gases in the second half of this century*". Reference is made in Article 5.1 to carbon sinks which should be conserved and enhanced.

Where adaptation is concerned, the agreement outlines numerous government actions to strengthen societies' ability to deal with the impacts of climate change and to provide continued and enhanced international support for adaptation to developing countries. These include financial support by developed countries, such as the ongoing collective goal to mobilise USD 100 billion per year until 2025 for adaptation and mitigation in developing regions, a figure which should be increased from 2025 onwards.

Intended Nationally Determined Contributions (INDCs)

Beyond the agreement itself, a number of the INDCs make reference to agriculture and food production. Of the 133 INDCs analysed by the Consultative Group of International Agricultural Research (CGIAR) in late November 2015, agricultural adaptation was referred to in 102 (94 of which included at least one adaptation measure), and targets related to agricultural mitigation were included in 103 (84 of which specified at least one mitigation measure).[2] Agricultural water management was included in 83 submissions.

The application of the INDCs will be supported by the Lima-Paris Action Agenda (LPAA). The LPAA features five major initiatives concerning agriculture. Initiatives include the *4 per 1000 Initiative: Soils for Food Security and Climate*, launched by state and non-state partners, which aims to protect and increase carbon stocks in soils, and the *Adaptation for Smallholder Agriculture Program* (ASAP), which intends to increase the climate resilience and food security of smallholder farmers.

Next steps

On 22 April 2016, the Paris Agreement was opened for signature for one year and was signed by 174 countries and the European Union. The agreement will enter into force after 55 countries that account for at least 55% of global emissions have deposited their instruments of ratification. Governments have agreed to meet every five years to take collective stock of the implementation of their strategies and to set more ambitious goals. The first formal global stocktaking dialogue will take place in 2023.

1. United Nations Framework Convention on Climate Change, http://unfccc.int/paris_agreement/items/9485.php
2. CGIAR, Research Program on Climate Change, Agriculture and Food Security, and CCAFS (November 2015), https://cgspace.cgiar.org/rest/bitstreams/62364/retrieve.

Market access

Since the 1994 Agreement on Agriculture, there have been significant improvements in market access. Reduced tariff levels occurred in line with country commitments under the agreement, and have also continued since. Since 2000, average applied agricultural tariffs have been in decline largely as a result of unilateral actions by some countries and a range of bilateral and regional trading agreements coming into force (Figure 2.9).

In absolute terms, since 2000 an increasing number of new bilateral and regional trade agreements (BRTAs) have been notified to the WTO each year (Figure 2.10). This has significantly increased the 'stock' of agreements in place and has resulted in an increasing proportion of world trade now being covered by these agreements – in 2014 only 7 WTO countries were not part of a notified and enforced bilateral or regional trade agreement. In 2008, slightly more than one-third of all world merchandise trade (excluding intra-European Union trade) was conducted within BRTAs, up from 18% in 1990 (WTO, 2011: 64). The share of global trade in agricultural products flowing between countries connected through BRTAs also grew from slightly above 20% in 1998 to nearly 40% in 2009 (OECD, 2013).

Despite the political sensitivity of the agricultural sector, a number of bilateral and regional trading agreements have made inroads into agricultural protection levels, providing for liberalisation beyond WTO levels. The OECD (2015a) found that in terms of market access, the majority of trade agreements have included tariff cuts and other market access concessions that exceed those of individual country WTO commitments. However, sensitive areas remain and for those products, market access provisions often reflect those at the multilateral level.

Bilateral and regional trade agreements also go beyond WTO commitments in other aspects. About a third of those agreements examined by OECD (2015a) incorporated obligations that went beyond areas covered in the WTO agreement on Agriculture. These are mostly related to provisions for technical assistance and are largely couched as best-endeavour provisions. A considerable number of agreements also crafted a WTO-plus framework for Sanitary and Phyto-Sanitary measures and for Technical Barriers to Trade, although in some cases these do not constitute enforceable obligations. Finally, over half of bilateral and regional agreements strengthen disciplines for export restrictions and subsidies, although these provisions are not exclusively geared towards agricultural products.

However, because of improvements in applied market access, considerable differences exist between applied and bound tariff levels. The binding overhang is largest in Norway and India where in both cases it amounts to nearly 80 percentage points. Moreover, large margins of binding overhang exist in both emerging and developed countries.

Figure 2.9. Applied agricultural tariff rates

Weighted average % 1996 to 2013

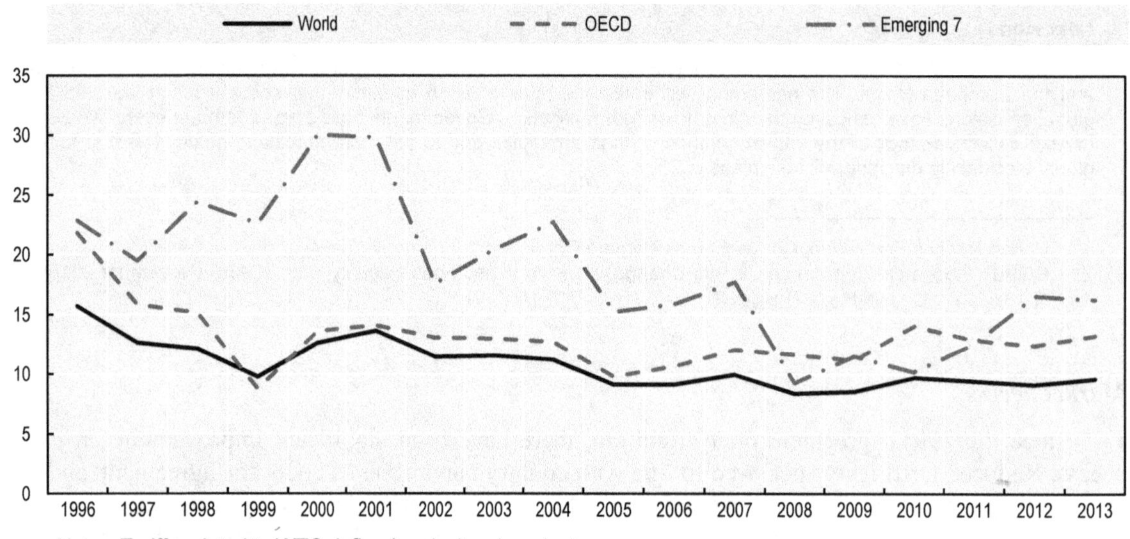

Notes: Tariffs related to WTO defined agricultural products.
Source: Author calculations based on WITS data (http://wits.worldbank.org/).

Figure 2.10. Notified bilateral and regional trade agreements

1957 to 2014

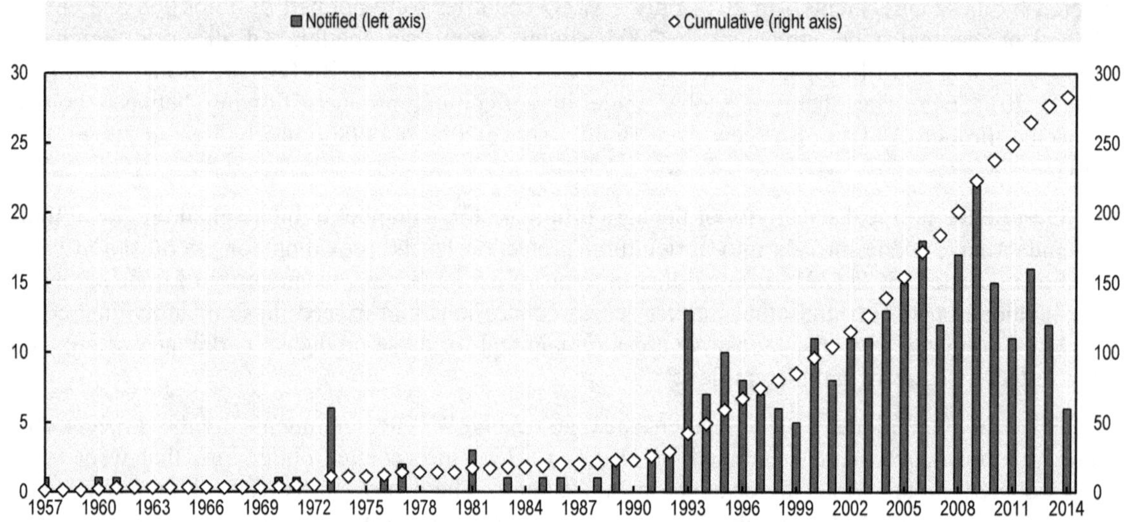

Source: WTO RTA database (www.wto.org/english/tratop_e/region_e/region_e.htm).

Across countries, tariffs placed on individual products may also vary considerably and differ substantially from average applied tariffs. The maximum duty applied to any particular agricultural product is in some instances several times larger than average applied tariffs. For example, in Norway and Switzerland, the maximum applied duty across agricultural products is more than 500%. Only Chile has a uniform schedule of tariffs, 6% for all products (unless covered by a bilateral or regional agreement). However, it should be noted that on its own, the level of a tariff can be misleading in terms of the actual protection offered. For example, in the case of tariff rate quotas, a very high out-of-quota tariff may confer no protection if the quota is sufficiently large so as not to be filled. In such an instance, the within quota tariff is important.

Apart from issues of specific products and significant binding overhang, there remain pockets of high applied tariffs. The landscape of these high applied tariffs levels has changed since 2000. Trends in high applied tariff levels, defined as those either 10 or 25 times or higher above the world agro-food average (simple average) in any given year, indicate that there has been an increase in the number of bilateral flows that are attracting high tariffs (Figure 2.11).[6] For example, in 2000 around 1 300 bilateral trade flows at the HS 6-digit level attracted applied duties that were at least ten times higher than the world average tariff applied to agro-food trade. By 2013, this had doubled to around 2 600 bilateral trade flows (a similar pattern exists for tariffs 25 times the agro-food average in any given year). Changes have, however, been variable. The cause of this is not clear as it could be driven by several factors (or a combination thereof). It could be a result of increased trading despite existing high tariff levels; increased tariffs on existing trade flows; falling global average tariffs; or simply reporting inconsistencies.

There is a relatively small set of countries that apply high tariffs to bilateral flows – those defined as 25 times the world agro-food average (Table 2.3). Across the period from 2000 to 2013, only 11 countries applied tariffs on agro-food products that were 25 or more times higher than the world agro-food average. For these countries, it is often a particular product set that attracts high tariffs rather than a broad application of high trade barriers. It should also be noted that in general, the trade values affected by high tariffs are low (with the caveat that high tariffs prevent trade flows and so does not represent potential trade value).[7] Further, the table shows only high rates of applied tariffs and does not include other potentially high rates of protection from specific tariffs or quotas.

Figure 2.11. Number of bilateral trade flows attracting high tariffs

2000 to 2013

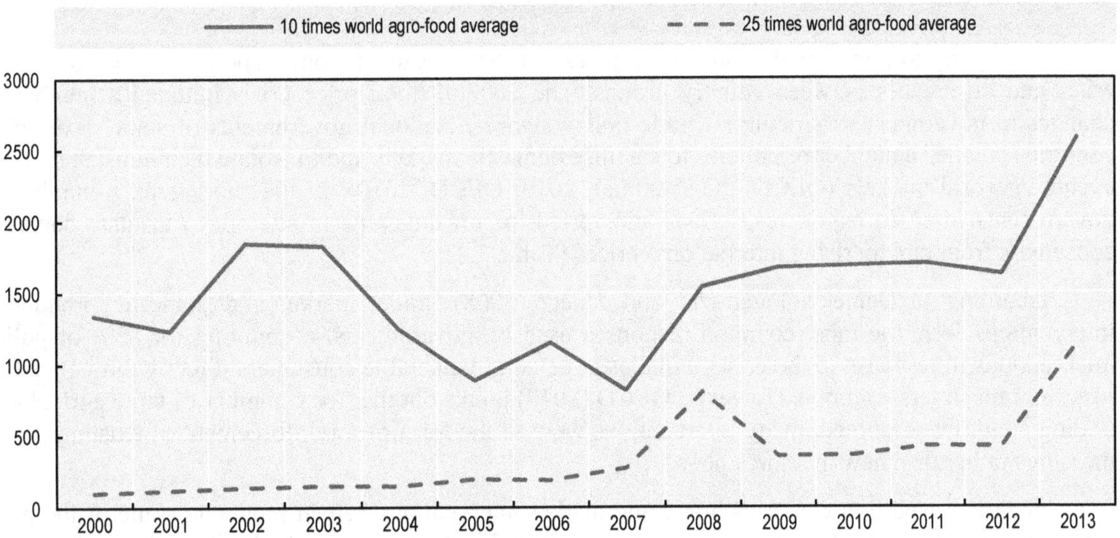

Source: Author calculations based on WITS data (http://wits.worldbank.org/).

Domestic support

There have been significant changes in domestic support since 2000, both across time and across countries. These have been driven by both a continuation of reforms began under the 1994 WTO Agreement on Agriculture and, importantly, in response to the food price spikes of 2007/08.

Global trends and the lasting effect of the food crisis

Overall measures of support – both the OECD producer support estimate (PSE) and the World Bank's nominal rate of assistance (NRA) – point to a fall in the level of support provided to agricultural producers worldwide. Average support levels across OECD countries fell from 32% of gross farm receipts in 2000 to 17% in 2014 (OECD, 2015b). Across all countries examined, NRA estimates of average total support to agriculture see a much smaller fall in the NRA from 0.29 in 2000 to 0.27 in 2011 (latest year available). When only major agricultural trading countries are considered (those shown in Tables 2.1 and 2.2), falls are significantly more dramatic – from 0.45 in 2000 to 0.29 in 2011.

Table 2.3. Countries applying tariffs 25 times world agro-food average

Total between 2000 to 2013

	Number of tariff lines 25 times world average	Average (simple) applied tariff on these flows	Share of trade affected over the period (%)
Egypt	1 414	1 705	0.81
Korea	2 273	446	1.07
Mexico	12	245	0.33
Morocco	54	322	0.10
Norway	404	329	0.10
Panama	20	371	0.01
Poland	39	370	0.02
St. Kitts and Nevis	4	400	>0.01
Chinese Taipei	19	343	>0.01
United States	106	350	>0.01
Zimbabwe	8	374	0.10

Notes: High tariff lines for Poland were applied prior to it joining the European Union in 2004. For Korea, the share of trade affected is likely to be overstated, see note 7.

Source: Author calculations based on WITS data (http://wits.worldbank.org/).

These point-to-point trends mask differences that have resulted from responses to the food price crisis and differences between country groups. The 2007/08 food price crisis initiated a number of changes to governments' agricultural trade policy stances. National governments of some developing countries pursued a number of policies to stabilise domestic markets and to isolate their consumers from events in world markets (OECD, 2009; Abbot, 2010; OECD, 2010). In the short term, a number of governments imposed export restrictions and varied import duties in an attempt to insulate domestic consumers from rapidly rising international prices (Table 2.4).

According to Demeke, Pangrazio and Maetz (2008), trade, market and domestic production interventions were the most common responses used by governments, accounting for 85% of policy interventions in response to the crisis. Policies targeted at vulnerable consumers directly through safety nets were much less common. However, OECD (2010) points out that for a number of large agricultural trading countries examined, many interventions were in the form of a reinforcement of existing policy measures rather than new measures per se.

For larger exporting countries, trade and market interventions helped moderate some of the price increases faced by domestic consumers (examples include wheat in China and India see – Galtier et al. (2013)). However, given such interventions were made by a number of countries, the cumulative effect of these on world prices meant that the effectiveness of such measures for any one country, particularly for smaller producers, was significantly lessened. Further, from an economy-wide perspective and over the longer term, the efficiency and effectiveness of ad hoc trade policy responses to manage domestic price variability is questionable and may work against food security (see OECD, 2015c; 2015d).

Anderson, Ivanic and Martin (2014) also found that trade and market intervention policies exaggerated overall price movements. Similarly, Headey (2011) suggests that trade policy related decisions were a major driver of the observed price spikes. For rice, wheat, maize and soybeans, trade actions by countries related to export restrictions, buying to increase stockholdings and removal of import restrictions.

Table 2.4. Trade-based policy measures commonly adopted in 2008

	Africa	Asia	Latin America	Overall
Countries surveyed	33	26	22	**81**
Market interventions				
Trade policy				
Reduction of tariffs and customs fees on imports	18	13	12	**43**
Restricted or banned export	8	13	4	**25**
Domestic market measures				
Suspension/reduction of VAT or other taxes	14	5	4	**23**
Released stocks at subsidised prices	13	15	7	**35**
Administered prices	10	6	5	**21**
Production support				
Production support	12	11	12	**35**
Production safety nets	6	4	5	**15**
Fertiliser and seed programs	4	2	3	**9**
Market Interventions	4	9	2	**15**
Consumer safety nets				
Cash transfers	6	8	9	**23**
Increase disposable income	4	8	4	**16**

Source: Demeke, Pangrazio and Maetz (2008).

The effects of these policies were particularly felt by net food importing countries that already had low trade barriers. The exaggerated price movements created by the application of insulation policies in other countries created worse outcomes than would have otherwise occurred. From a global perspective, the various individual country interventions, which were intended to improve food security, actually lessened it. Anderson, Ivanic and Martin (2014) found that trade based food price insulation policies implemented in 2007/08 could have actually increased the number of people living in poverty around the world.

In the period since, many countries have maintained a more defensive stance to international markets. Many have begun to pursue food self-sufficiency policies, often with reference to a desire to improve food security. The policy levers employed have varied, and many employ a raft of measures ranging from market price support provided by trade barriers, input subsidies and, for some, through the use of public stockholding programmes. Over the longer term, the use of such trade and domestic policies is likely to contribute to increasing future levels of price volatility in international markets as they export domestic price variation to the world market (Gouel, 2014). That said, some have also made use of less distortionary policies with significant investments in agricultural infrastructure and research and development.

The effects of the food crisis on domestic agricultural (and trade) policies can be seen in the NRA estimates (Figure 2.12). NRA rates were trending downwards prior to 2000 for both major agricultural trading countries and others. Part of the falling level of support has been argued to have been associated with rising food prices (nominal food price index shown on Figure 2.12). However, despite prices continuing to rise afterwards, there is a clear reversal in the trends toward falling rates of assistance.

It is also worth noting that support provided to agriculture in major trading countries (measured in terms of the NRA) is, on average, greater than that provided in other countries. Further, in terms of the policy responses to the food crisis, it appears that non-major trading countries had a greater proportional response than that of major trading countries.

Figure 2.12. Nominal rates of assistance: Contrasting trends

NRAs and food price index(2010 = 100) 2000 to 2011

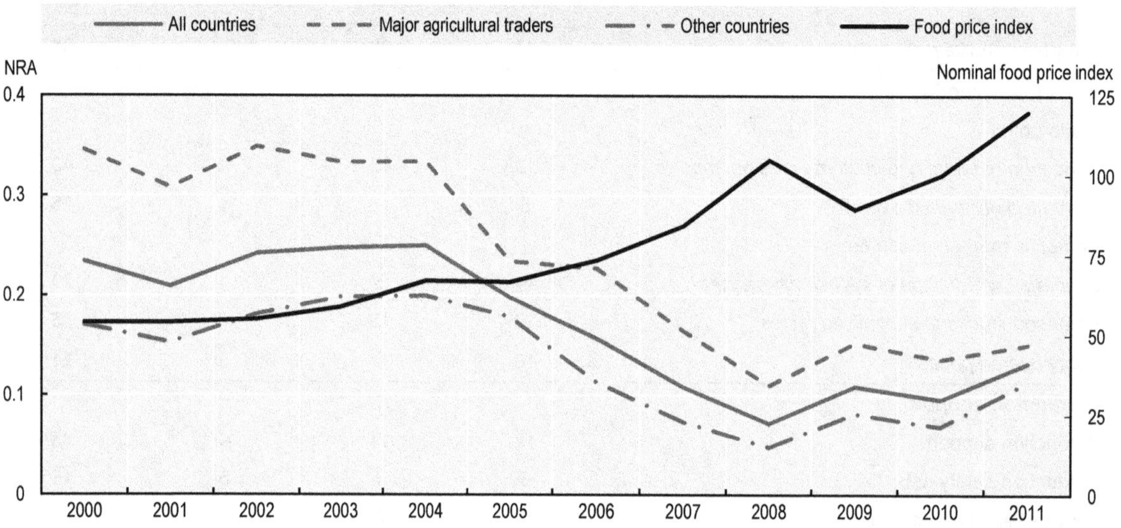

Notes: NRA estimates represent estimates for all (primary) Agriculture including non-product specific payments. Country level estimates obtained as value of production-weighted averages.

Source: World Bank (2012); Anderson and Valenzuela (2013); Anderson and Nelgen (2013); IMF IFS database (http://data.imf.org/).

Changing landscape of support

Increasingly, there appears to be a convergence in the use of producer policies by developed and emerging countries – in particular, those that directly support individual farmers (Figure 2.13). Since 1995, income transfers to individual farmers by some emerging and developing countries have been increasing, driven in part by rising levels of development and incomes within these countries, and for some, a push towards policies aimed at achieving self-sufficiency in particular agricultural products. In developed countries, a mix of reforms and changes in world food prices has played a role in the changes observed in the total levels of support.

PSE measured by the OECD show the contrasting developments between developed and emerging economies. In 1995, the eight emerging economies for which the OECD collects information on agricultural policies accounted for just under 5% of the total measured PSE (OECD and emerging economies). By 2014, these eight countries accounted for over 51% of the total.

Figure 2.13. Trends in PSE: OECD and emerging economies

Nominal PSE values 1995 to 2014 (USD billions)

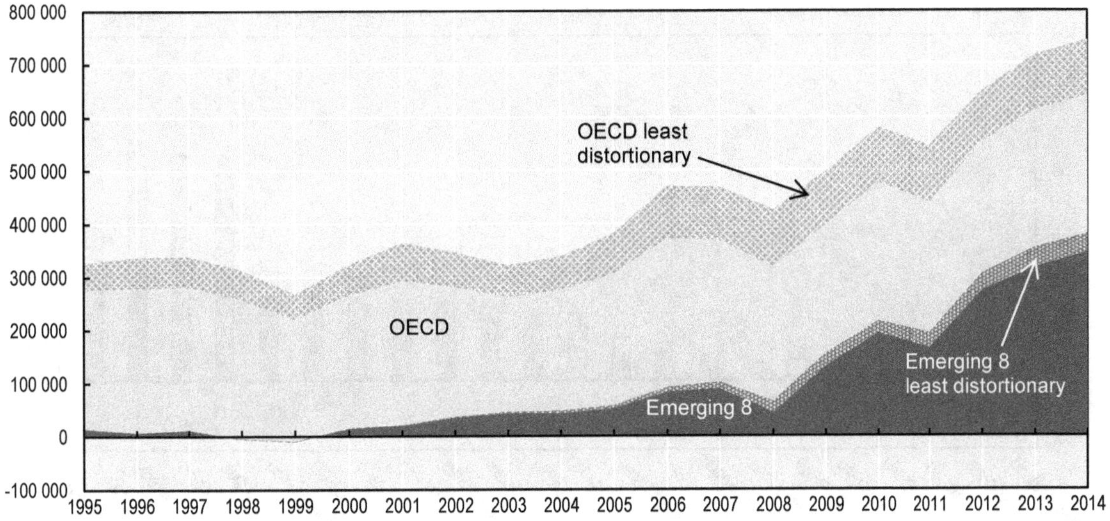

Notes: Least distortionary represent those payments that are decoupled from production and do not relate to inputs or outputs.

Source: Author estimates based on OECD Stat (http://stats.oecd.org/).

The makeup of the PSE has also changed since the 2000s (Figure 2.14). Within some emerging countries, notably Indonesia and China, the growth in PSE has been driven by a growth in the use of policies that are most distortionary in terms of their impact on trade – including market price support, output based payments and input subsidies. Other emerging economies, such as Brazil, show both a falling PSE and a shift towards decoupled payments. For many OECD countries, the share of the PSE made up of most distortionary policies has fallen since 2000 – most notably for the European Union where in 2014 around 68% of its support consisted of decoupled payments compared to around 35% in 2000. However, changes across OECD countries are not uniform, with Iceland, Japan, Korea, Switzerland and Norway maintaining high levels of support.

The change in the composition of support by some OECD countries has also been driven by changing objectives. For the European Union, for example, policies are increasingly focused on non-commodity outputs from the sector related to the environment and other objectives such as cultural landscapes, biodiversity and rural development.

Export competition

Actual use of export subsidies has also declined notably in recent years, in part as a result of high prices on international markets, but also as a result of policy reforms. Of the 18 WTO Members (counting all European Union member countries as one) that had agreed non-zero export subsidy commitments in the Uruguay Round, ten countries have not used export subsidies in all years notified since the beginning of the Doha Round in 2001. Of the remaining, three have reported continued use, and one, the United States, has only made limited use of export subsidies. In July 2013, the official decision to cut the export refund for poultry to zero (Commission Implementing Regulation (EU) No 689/2013), which for other meats like pork and beef was already the case, meant that, for the first time since the 1970s, no export subsidies would be paid on agricultural products. Further, at the latest WTO Ministerial Meeting (MC10), governments agreed to permanently remove agricultural export subsidies (Box 2.4).

Figure 2.14. Composition of the PSE

2000

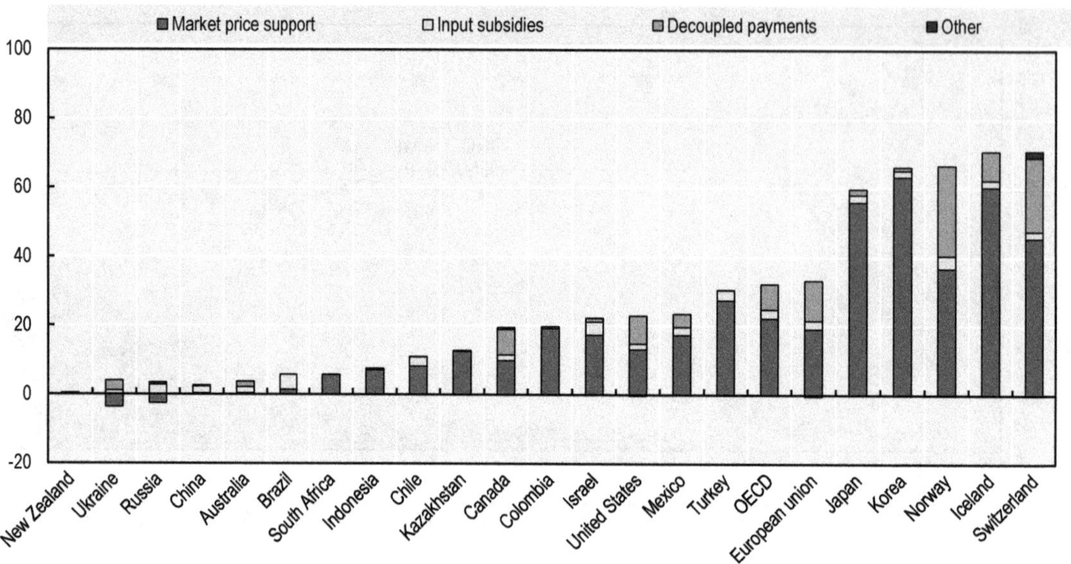

2014

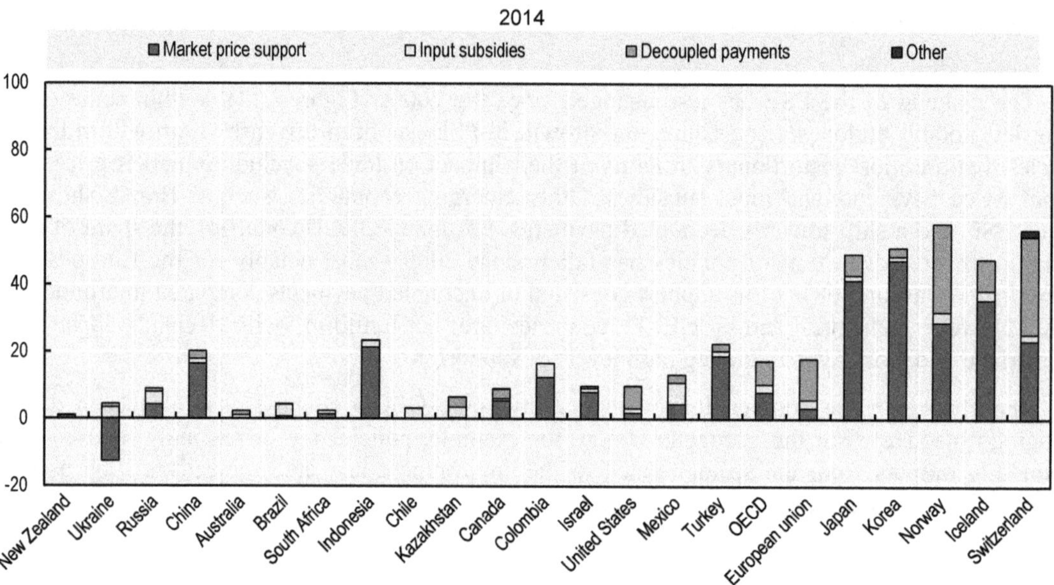

Source: Author estimates based on OECD Stat (http://stats.oecd.org/).

However, changes in other policy areas related to export competition that have similar effects on world trade are less clear. There is a lack of data on the subsidy equivalent of provisions relating to export financing, food aid and state trading enterprises making assessments of changes difficult. Despite this, based on notifications to the WTO, since the launch of the Doha round there appears to be some evidence to suggest positive developments in other areas of the export competition pillar (WTO, 2014a).

Box 2.4. Developments from WTO's MC10

On 19 December 2015 the WTO Tenth Ministerial Conference (MC10) in Nairobi, Kenya agreed on a package of Ministerial Decisions, a number of which are relevant to agriculture. The "Nairobi Package" includes a commitment to abolish export subsidies for farm exports, in addition to other agriculture-relevant decisions concerning public stockholding for food security purposes; a special safeguard mechanism (SSM) for developing countries; measures related to cotton; and preferential rules of origin.

Export subsidies: A key feature of the Nairobi Package is a Ministerial Decision on Export Competition, under which developed countries have pledged to eliminate subsidies for farm exports, with the exception of scheduled export subsidies for dairy and processed products and pork. The latter have been given more time and have been agreed to be phased out by the end of 2020. Developing countries have until the end of 2018 to phase out export subsidies, but will be able to continue to cover marketing and transport costs for agriculture exports until the end of 2023. The poorest and food-importing countries will be granted until the end of 2030 to meet their commitments.

In addition to the above, the decision contains restrictions, or "disciplines", to prevent the use of other export policies as subsidies. These disciplines include limitations on financing support for agriculture exporters, such as export credits, export credit guarantees or insurance programmes; rules for agricultural exporting state enterprises; and disciplines to ensure that international food aid does not adversely impact domestic markets.

Public stockholding for food security: The decision on Public Stockholding for Food Security Purposes reaffirms the commitment of WTO members to negotiate and make all concerted efforts to agree and adopt a "permanent solution" to this issue, which had been at the centre of discussions at the Bali Ministerial in 2013.

Cotton: The cotton decision calls on developed countries – and developing countries that declare themselves able to do so – to grant listed "cotton-related" exports from LDCs duty-free and quota-free access from 1 January 2016 onwards, to the extent provided for in their respective preferential trade agreements in favour of LDCs. Developed countries are also required to end cotton export subsidies immediately, while developing countries must do so by 1 January 2017. The decision also acknowledges reforms made by certain countries to their domestic cotton policies which may contribute to the reduction of domestic subsidies, while emphasising that further efforts need to be made.

Special Safeguard Mechanism (SSM): Countries agreed to maintain the right of developing countries to have recourse to a SSM based on import quantity and price triggers with precise arrangements to be further defined as envisaged under paragraph 7 of the Hong Kong Ministerial Declaration. Negotiations on an SSM will be pursued in the WTO Committee on Agriculture in Special Session in the context of addressing outstanding agricultural issues.

Other agriculture-relevant decisions at MC10 included a decision on preferential rules of origin for least developed countries. The decision states that when Members apply a processing criterion for agricultural goods they shall, to the extent provided for in their preference programme, allow the transformation of raw agricultural products into processed products to confer origin. Members are also asked to consider extending preferential treatment to products containing non-LDC originating materials of up to 75% of the final value of the product.

Source: WTO (2015), *Nairobi Package*, www.wto.org/english/thewto_e/minist_e/mc10_e/nairobipackage_e.htm.

With respect to food aid, its contribution to total official development assistance is marginal – around 3% – but it represents 18% of humanitarian assistance (Clay, 2014). In quantity terms, Clay (2014) reports that around 5 million tonnes is provided, of which between 80-90% is cereals. This represents around 8% of total LDC cereal imports, but only 0.5% of Net Food Importing Developing Country[8] imports. Food aid, including during the 2007/08 food crisis, has tended to be 'pro-cyclical'. That is, least available at times when prices are high and most available in the presence of low prices (Clay, 2012). This pattern suggests that at some level, food aid has an ongoing link with agricultural policy and delivery is subject to a time lag because of procedural issues. Despite this, moves away from the delivery of food to financial flows have created a downward trend in food aid quantities since 2000; albeit with a reversal of this trend between 2011 and 2012 (Figure 2.15).

At a broad level, the shift away from product based food aid may imply that the trade distorting risks have diminished since 2000. However, some have suggested the potential for trade distortions remains, with some commodities more at risk than others (Clay, 2014). Some of these risks stem from the United States retaining provisions within its 2014 Farm Bill around tying requirements, monetisation and surplus disposal. Others relate in particular to rice where donors predominately provide aid in the form of direct transfers (Brazil, Japan and the United States being the major donors).

Figure 2.15. Food aid: By type and delivery mode

Million tonnes, 2000 to 2012

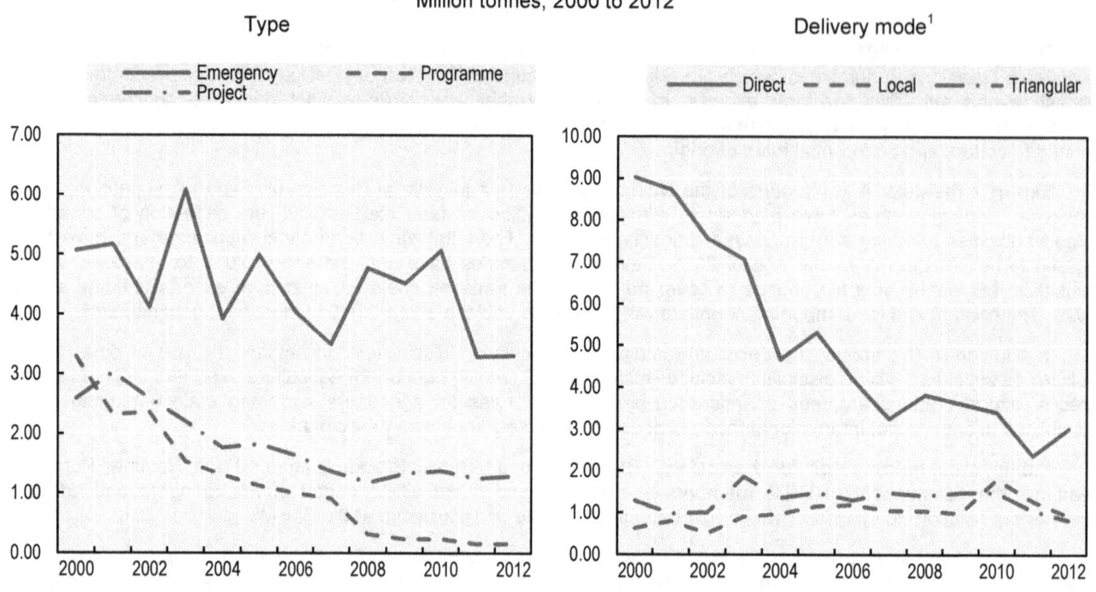

1. Direct is direct food transfer, local is when money is provided for food to be purchased on local markets, triangular represents purchases by donor country of third party food which is subsequently delivered to recipient country.

Source: WFP INTERFAIS (www.wfp.org/fais/).

With respect to state trading, recent research by the OECD, however, suggests that importing and exporting state trading enterprises in general may be increasingly competing with private firms (OECD 2015e). While not specific to agriculture, firms responding to the *OECD Business Survey on State Influence on* Competition *in International Markets* suggest that some state trading enterprises have been able to exploit a number of advantages of state ownership, influencing market outcomes (predominately through limiting sales).

The WTO reports that 20 members had reported 77 agricultural exporting state trading enterprises (WTO, 2014b; Díaz-Bonilla and Harris 2014). The countries with more state trading enterprises were China (25), India (14), and Colombia (14). Tobacco (21 STEs), other products (20), and fruits and vegetables (14) were the main items involved.[9]

In relation to export credits, little information exists on the significance of measured used by countries. In a recent survey of members on export competition, the WTO only had 36 responses to questions on export credits (including the European Union counted as one) (WTO, 2016a). Of the 36 countries who responded, 13 provided details on their export credit arrangements. For those which also provided time series data on expenditure, trends were mixed – some had expanding programmes while for others, programme expenditures were decreasing (WTO, 2016b).

Export restrictions

Although currently outside export competition arrangements, export restrictions on agricultural products have been used by some countries in an attempt to achieve domestic policy objectives. As discussed above, export restrictions and bans were used by some as temporary measures in response to the food price spikes on 2007/08 (Table 2.4). However, the use of such measures continues to and has affected trade in different commodities to varying degrees.

Table 2.5. Export restrictions on agricultural products

2007 to 2011

	Number of countries	Number of restrictions	Average share of production 2004-06	Share of production	Average share of exports 2004-06	Share of exports
			2007			
Rice	3	13	0.27	0.28	0.34	0.31
Wheat	5	14	0.28	0.29	0.24	0.24
Maize	1	3	0.03	0.03	0.16	0.15
Other grains	2	4.5	0.09	0.08	0.18	0.18
Soybeans	1	1.5	0.19	0.21	0.13	0.18
Other oilseeds	1	9	0.05	0.07	0.03	0.03
Vegetable oils	3	49.5	0.29	0.29	0.44	0.43
			2008			
Rice	8	39	0.71	0.71	0.52	0.48
Wheat	8	16	0.46	0.48	0.3	0.33
Maize	3	6.5	0.25	0.28	0.23	0.16
Other grains	3	4.5	0.12	0.12	0.26	0.31
Soybeans	2	2	0.26	0.22	0.14	0.08
Other oilseeds	2	1.5	0.13	0.07	0.05	0.03
Vegetable oils	4	38	0.28	0.1	0.41	0.42
			2009			
Rice	5	17	0.54	0.52	0.25	0.13
Wheat	3	6	0.3	0.34	0.12	0.05
Maize	1	0.5	0.03	0.03	0.16	0.17
Other grains	2	1	0.05	0.05	0.19	0.21
Soybeans	2	0.5	0.26	0.27	0.14	0.14
Other oilseeds	1	1	0.05	0.04	0.03	0.03
Vegetable oils	3	38	0.11	0.1	0.14	0.09
			2010			
Rice*	6	19	0.28	0.28	0.38	0.31
Wheat	7	8	0.29	0.3	0.24	0.17
Maize	4	3	0.04	0.05	0.18	0.21
Other grains	4	3.5	0.14	0.12	0.37	0.34
Soybeans	2	0.5	0.19	0.19	0.13	0.1
Other oilseeds	3	3.5	0.04	0.05	0.01	0.03
Vegetable oils	5	17	0.27	0.3	0.41	0.4
			2011			
Rice*	3	4	0.04	0.04	0.05	0.05
Wheat	6	6.5	0.13	0.15	0.22	0.31
Maize	3	2	0.04	0.06	0.18	0.3
Other grains	3	4.5	0.14	0.16	0.37	0.5
Soybeans	2	1	0.19	0.19	0.13	0.1
Other oilseeds	4	7.5	0.09	0.1	0.04	0.03
Vegetable oils	4	9.5	0.22	0.27	0.41	0.4

Notes: Each HS6 code counts as 1 if a restriction lasts more than six months and .5 if it lasts less than 6 months. * Information for rice in 2010 and 2011 excludes China since it is not clear how China's licenses were administered, and hence whether they were restrictive or not. In any year, average share of production or exports for 2004-06 refers to countries with policies in that year Data for other oilseeds include cottonseed, rapeseed, sunflower seed and palm kernel depending on the country and year Data for vegetable oils include soybean oil, rapeseed oil, sunflower seed oil, coconut oil, palm kernel oil, palm oil, cottonseed oil depending on the country and year. Data are not available for all relevant commodities for all countries. See OECD (2014) for more detail.

Source: OECD (2014).

Data collected by the OECD suggests that the use of such measures persisted over the period from 2007 to 2011 (Table 2.5). Further, these export restrictions (including Argentina's export tax arrangements) have been used across a range of agro-food export products. Across the selected years shown in Table 2.5 more countries consistently place restrictions on the trade of rice and wheat. However, in terms of the number of restrictions, more are applied to trade in vegetable oils, followed by rice and wheat.

When examining the proportion of total world trade that was potentially affected by export restrictions, it is again trade in rice, wheat and vegetable oils that were most affected. On average over the five-year period for which data is presented, export restrictions were imposed by countries that accounted for between 21% and 37% of total exports of these three products.[10]

Notes

1. For more information on the updated database see www.gtap.agecon.purdue.edu/databases/v9/default.asp.
2. To some extent, non-tariff, behind the border barriers and other policy factors that limit agricultural trade between two nations will already be captured in the trade flows and thus export and import shares of any given country. As such, this analysis assumes separability in the effects of border and domestic support measures and those of other non-tariff and behind the border barriers not included in this analysis. Further, as the type of general equilibrium modelling employed does not allow for new bilateral trade flows to be created – even if based on price alone, trade potential exists (that is, if two countries did not trade in a particular product before the reform, they will also not trade after) – it is assumed that the reasons for no trade are non-price related that will in part be related to the modelled frictions to international trade.
3. The *OECD/FAO Outlook* is updated annually with latest medium term projects available at: www.agri-outlook.org/.
4. Estimates represent compound annual growth rates in the real value of reported agricultural product imports and exports respectively, based on Comtrade data for the period between 1994 and 2013.
5. Typically used to measure the concentration of incomes, a Gini coefficient of 1 represents a situation of complete concentration where there is only one exporter or importer, with 0 representing a situation where all have equal amounts of either exports or imports.
6. Trends in applied tariff levels are complicated by country reporting. There is significant variability in the levels of tariff reporting by WTO countries, meaning gaps in any given year exist. These gaps influence the results obtained. The results represent the number of tariff lines where the reported applied tariff rate exceeded 10 or 25 times the simple world average. As such, no specific accounting for tariff rate quotas, in or out of quota rates, has been made.
7. In the data, an exception exists for Korea where there is significant trade in maize despite high tariffs. However, much of the imports of maize occur within the duty free limits of the tariff-rate-quotas applied and as such, these values have been excluded from Table 3. Similarly, Korea also imports supplementary feeds, fodder roots and mixed feeds under similar arrangements. However, the nature of the data does not allow these to be separated out so the share of trade affected is likely to be overstated.
8. Net Food Importing Developing Countries are a grouping of countries within the WTO framework that depend on food imports for their food supply. Countries within this grouping are eligible as beneficiaries in respect to the measures provided within the *Marrakesh Ministerial Decision on Measures Concerning the Possible Negative Effects of the Reform Programme on Least-Developed and Net Food-Importing Developing Countries*. The group has varied in

composition over time and, as of the last update of the listing in 2012, consisted of all least developed countries defined by the United Nations along with 31 other nations (WTO document no. G/AG/5/Rev.10, 23 March 2012, www.wto.org/english/tratop_e/agric_e/ag_work_e.htm).

9. Reporting on state-owned enterprises under Article XVII is not always comprehensive or timely and as such results are not always likely to be accurate.

10. The three-year period chose represents the average export share between 2004 and 2006. This period represents a period before most countries began restricting exports. A three-year average for production and exports is shown to reduce climatic and other particularities of any one year. For the countries and commodities represented, the period 2004 to 2006 is assumed to be representative of a "typical" year before the more frequent use of export restrictions during 2007-11. More information can be found in OECD (2014).

References

Abbot, P. (2010), "Stabilisation Policies in Developing Countries after the 2007-08 Food Crisis", Background paper to the OECD Global Forum on Agriculture: Policies for Agricultural Development, Poverty Reduction and Food Security, 29-30 November 2010, Paris.

Anderson, K., M. Ivanic and W. Martin (2014), "Food Price Spikes, Price Isolation, and Poverty", *Policy Research Working Paper*, No. 7011, World Bank, Washington, DC.

Anderson, K. and E. Valenzuela (2013), *Estimates of Distortions to Agricultural Incentives, 1955-2011 (updated June 2013)*, World Bank, Washington, DC, available at www.worldbank.org/distortions.

Anderson, K. and S. Nelgen (2013), *Updated Database of National and Global Distortions to Agricultural Incentives, 1955 to 2011*, World Bank, Washington, DC.

Brink, L. (2014), *Commitments under the WTO Agreement on Agriculture and the Doha Draft Modalities: How do they Compare to Current Policy?*, Background paper to the OECD Global Forum on Agriculture: Issues in Agricultural Trade Policy, 2 December 2014, Paris.

CGIAR (2015), *Research Program on Climate Change, Agriculture and Food Security, and CCAFS*, CGIAR, Montpellier, https://cgspace.cgiar.org/rest/bitstreams/62364/retrieve.

Clay, E. (2014), "Trade Policy Options for Enhancing Food Aid Effectiveness: Revisiting the Draft Doha Deal", in R. Meléndez-Ortiz; C. Bellmann and J. Hepburn (eds.), *Tackling Agriculture in the Post-Bali Context*, International Centre for Trade and Sustainable Development, Geneva, Switzerland.

Clay, E. (2012), "Trade Policy Options for Enhancing Food Aid Effectiveness", *Issue Paper 41*, International Centre for Trade and Sustainable Development, Geneva, Switzerland, www.ictsd.org.

Commission Implementing Regulation (EU) "No 689/2013 of 18 July 2013 Fixing the Export Refunds on Poultrymeat", *Official Journal of the European Union*, L 196, 19.7.2013, pp. 13-15.

Demeke, M., G. Pangrazio and M. Maetz (2008), *Country Responses to the Food Security Crisis: Nature and Preliminary Implications of the Policies Pursued*, Agricultural Policy Support Service, FAO, Rome.

Díaz-Bonilla, E. and J. Harris (2014), "Export Subsidies and Export Credit", *Tackling Agriculture in the Post-Bali Context,* International Centre for Trade and Sustainable Development, Geneva.

Disdier, A-C., L. Fontagné and M. Mimouni (2008), "The Impact of Regulations on Agricultural Trade: Evidence from the SPS and TBT Agreements", *American Journal of Agricultural Economics*, Vol. 90/2, Oxford University Press, Oxford, pp. 336-350.

FAO Stat. (2016), *FAOSTAT*, Food and Agriculture Organization of the United Nations Statistics Division, Rome, http://faostat3.fao.org/home/E.

Galtier, F., B. Vindel and P. Timmer (2013), "Managing food Price Instability in Developing Countries: A Critical Analysis of Strategies and Instruments", Agence Française de Développement, Paris.

Gouel, C. (2014), "Trade Policy Coordination and Food Price Volatility", *CEPII Working Paper*, No. 2014-23, CEPII, Paris.

Headey, D. (2011), "Rethinking the Global Food Crisis: The Role of Trade Shocks", *Food Policy*, Vol. 36, Elsevier, Amsterdam, pp. 136-46.

IMF IFS database (2016), *IMF Data*, International Monetary Fund, Washington D.C. www.imf.org/en/Data.

Li, Y. and J.C. Beghin (2012), "A Meta-Analysis of Estimates of the Impact of Technical Barriers to Trade", *Journal of Policy Modeling*, Vol. 31/ 6, Elsevier, Amsterdam, pp. 497-511.

Naylor, R. L. and W. P. Falcon (2010), "Food Security in an Era of Economic Volatility", *Population and Development Review*, Vol. 35/4, Wiley, New Jersey, pp. 693-723.

OECD Stat (2016), *OECD Agriculture Statistics*, Organisation for Economic Co-operation and Development, Paris, http://stats.oecd.org/BrandedView.aspx?oecd_bv_id=agr-data-en&doi=83ff9179-en.

OECD (2015a), "Regional Trade Agreements and Agriculture", *OECD Food, Agriculture and Fisheries Papers*, No. 79, OECD Publishing, Paris, http://dx.doi.org/10.1787/5js4kg5xjvvf-en.

OECD (2015b), *Agricultural Policy Monitoring and Evaluation 2015*, OECD Publishing, Paris, http://dx.doi.org/10.1787/agr_pol-2015-en.

OECD (2015c), *Issues in Agricultural Trade Policy: Proceedings of the 2014 OECD Global Forum on Agriculture*, OECD Publishing, Paris, http://dx.doi.org/10.1787/9789264233911-en.

OECD (2015d), *Managing Food Insecurity Risk: Analytical Framework and Application to Indonesia*, OECD Publishing, Paris, http://dx.doi.org/10.1787/9789264233874-en.

OECD (2015e), "International Trade and Investment by State Enterprises", *OECD Trade Policy* Papers, by Kowalski, P. and K. Perepechay, OECD Publishing, Paris, http://dx.doi.org/10.1787/5jrtcr9x6c48-en.

OECD (2014), "How Export Restrictive Measures Affect Trade in Agricultural Commodities" by Liapis, P. in OECD *Export Restrictions in Raw Materials Trade: Facts, Fallacies and Better Practices*, OECD Publishing, Paris.

OECD (2013), "The Impact of Regional Trade Agreements on Trade in Agricultural Products", by Bureau, J. and S. Jean in *OECD Food, Agriculture and Fisheries Papers*, No. 65, OECD Publishing, Paris, http://dx.doi.org/10.1787/5k3xznkz60vk-en.

OECD (2012), *Evaluation of Agri-environmental Policies: Selected Methodological Issues and Case Studies*, OECD Publishing, Paris, http://dx.doi.org/10.1787/9789264179332-en.

OECD (2010), "Policy Responses in Emerging Economies to International Agricultural Commodity Price Surges", by Jones, D. and A. Kwieciński in *OECD Food, Agriculture and Fisheries Papers*, No. 34, OECD Publishing, Paris, http://dx.doi.org/10.1787/5km6c61fv40w-en.

OECD (2009), "Development Dimensions of High Food Prices", by Abbott, P. in *OECD Food, Agriculture and Fisheries Papers*, No. 18, OECD Publishing, Paris, http://dx.doi.org/10.1787/222521043712.

OECD (2008a), "Rising Food Prices: Causes and Consequences", *OECD Policy Brief*, OECD Publishing, Paris, www.oecd.org/dataoecd/54/42/40847088.pdf.

OECD (2008b), "Agricultural Policy Design and Implementation: A Synthesis", by van Tongeren, F. in *OECD Food, Agriculture and Fisheries Papers*, No. 7, OECD Publishing, Paris, http://dx.doi.org/10.1787/243786286663.

OECD-Food and Agriculture Organization of the United Nations (2015), *OECD-FAO Agricultural Outlook 2015*, OECD Publishing, Paris, http://dx.doi.org/10.1787/agr_outlook-2015-en.

Piesse, J. and C. Thirtle (2009), "Three Bubbles and a Panic: And Explanatory Review of Recent Food Commodity Price Events", *Food Policy*, Vol. 34, Elsevier, Amsterdam, pp. 119-29.

United Nations (2016), *United Nations Framework Convention on Climate Change*, United Nations, New York City, http://unfccc.int/paris_agreement/items/9485.php

WFP INTERFAIS (2016), *Food Aid Information System*, World Food Programme, Rome, www.wfp.org/fais/.

Winchester, N. (2009), "Is There a Dirty Little Secret? Non-Tariff Barriers and the Gains from Trade", *Journal of Policy Modeling*, Vol. 31/ 6, Elsevier, Amsterdam, pp. 819-834.

WITS (2016), *World Integrated Trade Solution*, The World Bank, Washington D.C. , http://wits.worldbank.org/default.aspx.

World Bank (2012), *Distortions to Agricultural Incentives*, World Bank, Washington, DC, available at: http://go.worldbank.org/5XY7A7LH40.

WTO (2016a), "Export Subsidies, Export Credits, Export Credit Guarantees or Insurance Programmes, International Food Aid and Agricultural Exporting State Trading Enterprises", Background Document by the Secretariat, Document G/AG/W/125/Rev.4, 11 May 2016, WTO, Geneva.

WTO (2016b), "Export Subsidies, Export Credits, Export Credit Guarantees or Insurance Programmes, International Food Aid and Agricultural Exporting State Trading Enterprises: Export Credits, Export Credit Guarantees or Insurance Programmes Addendum", Background Document by the Secretariat, Document G/AG/W/125/Rev.4/Add.2, 11 May 2016, WTO, Geneva.

WTO (2015), *Nairobi Package*, WTO, Geneva, www.wto.org/english/thewto_e/minist_e/mc10_e/nairobipackage_e.htm.

WTO (2014a), "Annual Export Competition Review: Submission from the Cairns Group to the 74th Meeting of the Committee on Agriculture (COA) in June 2014", Document G/AG/W/129, 2 June 2014, WTO, Geneva.

WTO (2014b), "Background Document on Export Subsidies, Export Credits, Export Credit Guarantees or Insurance Programmes, International Food Aid and Agricultural Exporting State Trading Enterprises", G/AG/W/125 and annexes, 21 May 2014, WTO, Geneva.

WTO (2011), *World Trade Report 2011: The WTO and Preferential Trade Agreements: From Co-existence to Coherence*, WTO, Geneva.

WTO RTA database (2016), *Regional Trade Agreements Information System (RTA-IS)*, WTO, Geneva, http://rtais.wto.org/UI/PublicMaintainRTAHome.aspx.

Chapter 3

Impacts of current agricultural policies and potential impacts from reform

This chapter explores the impacts of current agricultural domestic support and trade policies on markets and countries along with a number of scenarios looking at both reforms and increases in protection. First, the chapter sets out the modelling approach used in the study. Second, the impacts of current policies on production, trade and the economy are presented. Third, a closer look at the impacts of current policies on individual international agricultural markets and prices is presented. Fourth, the chapter presents possible multilateral reform scenarios, including one of increased protection.

The statistical data for Israel are supplied by and under the responsibility of the relevant Israeli authorities. The use of such data by the OECD is without prejudice to the status of the Golan Heights, East Jerusalem and Israeli settlements in the West Bank under the terms of international law

3.1 Introduction

The modelling of the impacts of policies on markets and economic activity invariably requires a number of assumptions to be made. Moreover, characteristics of particular policies, or a lack of information on the economic effects of policies, add further complexity to the task. These factors often reduce the analysis of policy impacts to a narrower set of policy variables. This study is no different. That said, there have been significant developments within this narrower set of policies, which coupled with changes in markets warrants a re-inspection of the potential distortions created in agricultural markets.

This chapter sets out the modelling approach used and the results of the assessment of current agricultural policies along with a number of reform scenarios.

3.2 Modelling the impacts of agricultural policies and potential impacts from reform

The modelling of policy impacts and reform scenarios concentrates on border measures (tariffs, quotas and export taxes and subsidies) and domestic support policies (Box 3.1). The general equilibrium effects of policies and reform are explored through the OECD METRO model (Box 3.2). METRO is a CGE model designed to analyse trade policies. Market level impacts on world prices and trading patterns are explored through the OECD-FAO AGLINK-COSIMO model.

Box 3.1. What policy measures are modelled?

In the scenarios used in the study, the policy measures explicitly modelled include:

- domestic support to agriculture in the form of subsidies/taxes paid to land
- domestic support to agriculture in the form of subsidies/taxes paid to labour
- domestic support to agriculture in the form of subsidies/taxes paid to intermediate inputs into agricultural production
- domestic support to agriculture in the form of subsidies/taxes paid on outputs
- tariffs applied to, and ad valorem equivalents of all quota arrangements on, agro-food products and selected processed agricultural products (dairy, sugar and vegetable oils and fats)
- export subsidies applied to agricultural products and selected processed agricultural products (dairy, sugar and vegetable oils and fats).

METRO breaks down production and trade of commodities according to use – intermediate, household, government and capital consumption. The differentiation of commodity supply, and thus the resulting trade flows, by use category improves the ability to depict and analyse, amongst other things, global value chains through relative changes in intermediate final goods trade, allowing for a more nuanced understanding of the possible impacts of trade reform.

The model has a number of elements related to market access (tariffs and tariff equivalents) and domestic support making it well suited for the analysis of agricultural reform. The model structure is described in detail in OECD (2015).

The METRO database employed in this study is based on the GTAP 9 database, with a base year of 2011. As such, all estimates derived are in constant 2011 USD terms. For this analysis, it has been assumed that the balance of payments for a given country remains fixed after the policy shock, meaning that changes in the real exchange rate occur in response to any changes in the prices of exports or imports. Government balance is assumed constant and expenditure predefined. The government balances income changes by variation of the income tax rate. The volume of investment is fixed and savings adjust to investment, all factors are fully employed and mobile across sectors.

Box 3.2. About the METRO model

The OECD Trade Model, METRO, is a computable general equilibrium (CGE) model derived from the Social Accounting Matrix (SAM) based CGE model GLOBE developed by Scott McDonald, Karen Thierfelder and Terrie Walmsley (McDonald et al., 2013) using GAMS software. The model is a direct descendant of an early United States Department of Agriculture model (Robinson et al., 1990) and NAFTA (Robinson et al., 1993) and follows trade principles from the 1-2-3 model (de Melo and Robinson, 1989; Devarajan et al., 1990). Namely, these models divide an economy into tradable and non-tradable goods and link domestic and world prices through the tradable sectors. The model is calibrated using an augmented Social Accounting Matrix (SAM) version of the GTAP database (for v8 see Narayanan et al., 2012).

The novelty and strength of METRO lies in the detailed trade structure and the differentiation of production and consumption commodities by use – intermediate, household, government and capital consumption. The differentiation of commodity supply, and thus the resulting trade flows, by use category improves the ability to depict and analyse, amongst other things, global value chains (GVCs). In addition, this structure allows the modelling of policy instruments targeting specific uses, such as resource-based restrictions, local content requirements, and government consumption.

The model is based on a series of regional SAMs, derived from the GTAP database, linked through trade relationships. This database identifies agents (households, production units and government) and serves as a base to which to calibrate the model. In addition, the database contains a series of elasticities, including substitution elasticities governing the interaction of imports or exports and domestic commodities, the Constant Elasticity of Substitution (CES) elasticities of the production functions, income elasticities of demand and the Frisch (marginal utility of income) parameter. Finally, the database contains taxes and tariff information on a national and bilateral basis, respectively

Source: OECD (2015), www.oecd.org/officialdocuments/publicdisplaydocumentpdf/?cote=TAD/TC/WP(2014)24/FINAL&docLanguage=En).

The scenarios explored

To assess the impacts of current policies and reforms, a number of scenarios have been explored.

1. Assessing the **current impacts** of policy measures: this scenario explores the impacts of the application of current tariffs and quotas, export subsidies and production distorting domestic support (see Box 3.1) across all agricultural markets (23 regions, 26 sectors and 9 value added factors were modelled – see Annex 3.A1 for full list). The base year for analysis is 2011 and so the scenario represents the policies and market conditions of that time with the exception of export subsidies in the European Union which are taken as zero (this also applies for the scenarios described in ii and iii). The simulation is set up as counterfactual, removing all agro-food measures. It does not explore changes in other policies such as non-tariff measures, behind the border barriers, export restrictions and credits or state trading.

2. Exploring the impacts from **trade and domestic policy reform** that might feasibly be achieved via a multilateral agreement at the WTO, in terms of improvements in market access and a reduction in domestic support. The complete removal of agricultural tariffs and the complete winding back of domestic support is an unrealistic proposition for any possible multilateral reform effort. However, it could be expected that some reform to these arrangements is possible. Whilst keeping away from assessments of past and possible specific modalities, some insights can be gained into possible effects of multilateral reform by examining a stylised reform scenario. This scenario represents a situation where modest effort is made in reforming distortions to agricultural markets through the multilateral system. The scenario depicts both changes to border barriers (tariffs and quotas) and domestic support. The success that has already been achieved at MC10 with the removal of export subsidy (see Box 3.3 for further details) is included in part with the exception that European Union subsidies are already removed in the base. The reform scenario assumes:

    - Tariffs (and tariff equivalents for quotas and tariff-quotas) on all agro-food products in developed countries (excluding Japan) being reduced by a uniform 50% with the same cut applied to domestic support.[1] Export subsidies, where relevant, are set to zero. For certain developed countries, some sectors are subjected to smaller levels of reform with:

- Tariffs (and tariff equivalents for quotas and tariff-quotas) on all agro-food products in Japan being reduced by a uniform 25% with a similar cut to domestic support. Rice is exempted and only a 5% cut applied.
- Sugar in the United States is exempted and only a 5% cut applied.
- Dairy is exempted in Canada and only a 5% cut applied.

- Tariffs (and tariff equivalents for quotas and tariff-quotas) on all agro-food products in all other countries being reduced by a uniform 10% with the same cut applied to domestic support. Export subsidies are, where relevant, set to zero.
- As an extension to this scenario, the situation where developing countries apply the same cuts as developed – that is a 50% cut instead of 10% – is explored. This extension is referred to as "**policy reform all**".

3. Exploring the impacts of a "**policy drift**" scenario which compares a situation where an agreement is reached that locks in current levels of *applied market access* and *domestic support* to a situation where interventions in agro-food markets increase (both in terms of reducing market access and increases in production and trade distorting support). This scenario effectively represents an agreement on removing the difference between bound and applied tariff levels and maintains current rates of domestic support – that is, it maintains the status quo in terms of agriculture trade and domestic support policy. The policy drift scenario is then defined as a situation where tariffs (and tariff equivalents for quotas and tariff-quotas) on agro-food products increase by 25% in the People's Republic of China (hereafter "China"),[2] Indonesia, India, Malaysia and the Russian Federation with increases in domestic support based on changes that have been seen in the PSE for China and Indonesia over the period between 2011 and 2014 (with the average applied to the remaining as PSE estimates do not exist). For all other countries, the status quo is maintained. Specifically, this means that for:

- China, where PSE estimates have increased from 10.3% to 20.2%, a 100% increase in output subsidies is applied. Domestic support provided to production inputs is increased by 30% in line with actual changes.
- Indonesia, where PSE estimates have increased from 15.1% to 23.3%, a 54% increase in output and input subsidies is applied.
- The Russian Federation, where PSE estimates show a fall from 14.9% to 8.9%, output and input subsidies are kept the same which assumes that domestic support has increased by 67% compared with the support it provided in 2011.
- India and Malaysia, the average PSE increase for the group is applied which represents a 50% increase in output and input subsidies applied to agriculture.

In assessing the current impacts of agricultural policies, both the METRO and AGLINK-COSIMO models have been used. The METRO model has been used to assess the other reform scenarios. The AGLINK-COSIMO is used to assess to assess the impacts on prices in key agricultural commodity markets. In all scenarios, a range of sensitivity tests on parameters and market clearing assumptions have been conducted (details are set out in the appendixes).

Recent developments in agricultural markets make the policy drift scenario relevant. OECD PSE estimates for some emerging economies show a trend towards increased domestic support (Chapter 2). Further, recent actions by countries such as Indonesia show that unilateral increases in tariffs across of a range of agricultural products are a real possibility – particularly as the focus on self-sufficiency for food security is a facet of the domestic policy settings of a number of countries.

Box 3.3. Benefits from locking in the removal of export subsidies

With the agreement reached at MC10 on export subsidies (Box 2.4) it is worth exploring the possible benefits from the agreements to remove export subsidies for agricultural products. One of the more significant changes witnessed since 2001 has been the reduction in, and even removal of, a number of export subsidies. These changes, in part, reflect high prices on international markets, but are also as a result of policy reforms.

The agreement reached at the WTO should both foster further reforms to allow world markets to function more efficiently, but also help 'future proof' the world trading system. With pressures on agricultural production systems growing from increasing populations, changing consumer tastes on the back of rising incomes, and uncertain impacts from climate change, locking in the removal of export subsidies should provide significant benefits and increase the resilience of world agricultural markets, and, ultimately the resilience of world food supplies.

The challenges of climate and rising demand will mean that, in future, more consumers will rely on internationally sourced products to meet their food needs. This will be either through the direct provision of final consumption goods, or through intermediate products delivered to global value chains. World markets will need to deliver messages to producers through prices so that production occurs in areas where it is most efficient and sustainable to do so, and so that it can respond and move in reaction to changing climates. The removal of export subsidies should aid in addressing these challenges.

Figure 3.1. Production and trade effects of selected products

Contribution to overall % change

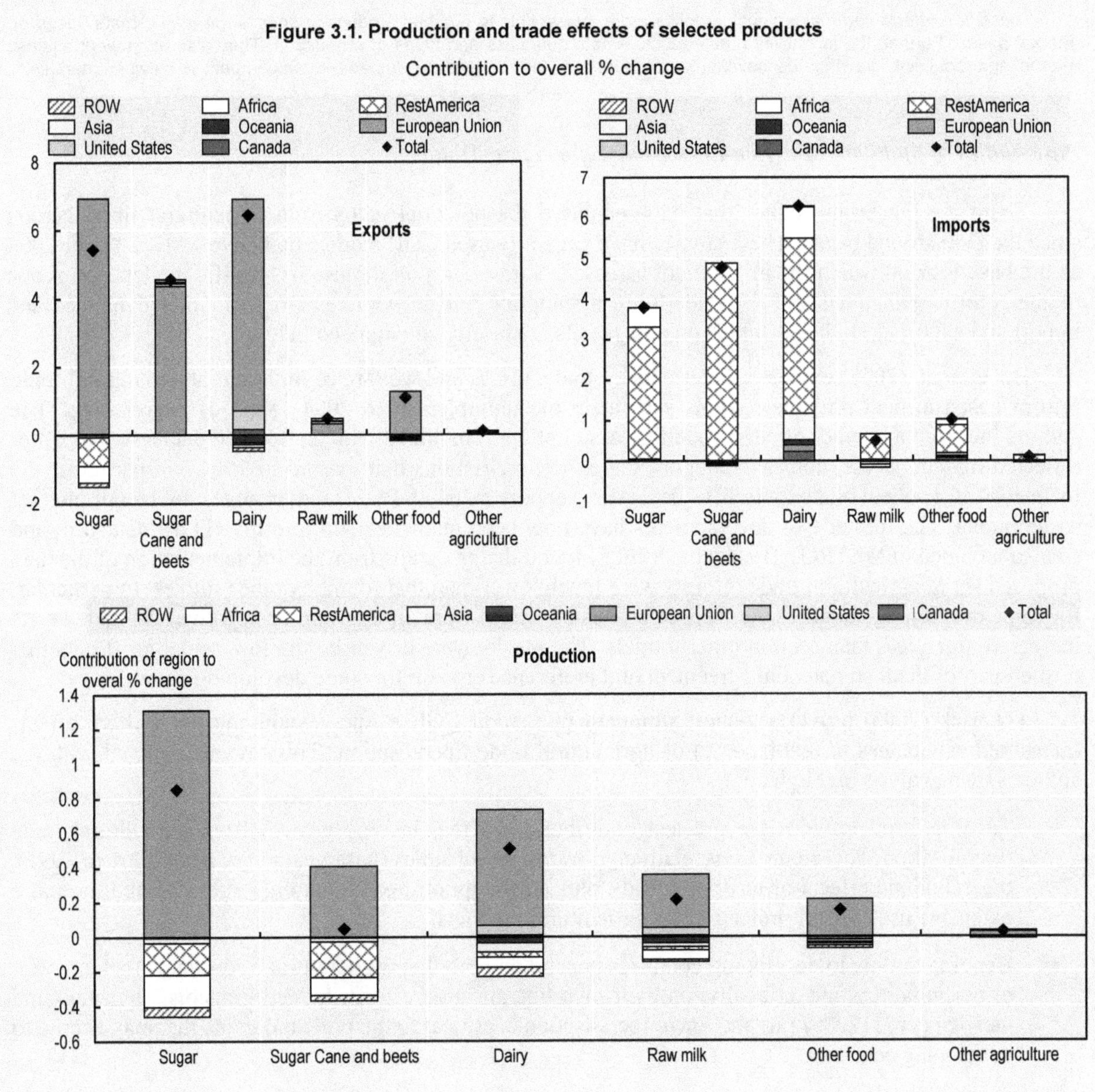

Box 3.3. Benefits from locking in the removal of export subsidies (cont.)

The effects of export subsidy removal to help address future challenges for agricultural markets are best assessed by looking at the effects of returning to past levels of export subsidies. Assuming the European Union, United States and Canada were to increase export subsidies to 2004 levels, we would see a number of effects on world markets. As expected, world prices for some commodities would fall, production would become more concentrated in subsidising countries, exports from other regions would fall as would production of a number of commodities.

Artificially lower prices limit the development of agricultural production in a number of regions. While in the short term consumers may benefit from lower prices, in the long term the costs of missed opportunities for production in areas of relatively greater productivity imposes costs on these consumers. Importantly, it limits the potential for agricultural income growth, often in the poorest regions of the world. Producing more in regions where costs are greater also means that globally the food system is higher cost than it otherwise would be.

While the effects on individual markets and economies differ, both in the short and long run, the use of export subsidies is also likely to decrease the flexibility of global production systems in meeting the challenges brought by climate change and rising demand. With the use of subsidies, production becomes more centred in specific areas in the world and becomes less responsive to changes in price.

These two effects can make global supplies more susceptible to regional production shocks, be they climate based or market based. Further, the incentives created lock-in both quantities and types of production. They also often work against promoting productivity growth and innovation as producers no longer need to adapt to remain competitive on world markets.

Past studies of multilateral agricultural trade reform post-Doha

There are numerous studies that have analysed the potential gains from agricultural liberalisation since the Doha round began. These studies have generally used CGE models that have 1997, 2001 or 2004 as the base year on which the impacts are assessed. Studies vary in the use of specific models, the scope of the reforms examined and the underlying assumptions made with respect to market dynamics and import and export elasticities. Details on past results are briefly summarised below.

Bouët et al. (2005) explored the effects on trade, prices and welfare of multilateral agricultural trade reform based around possible reforms set out in the unimplemented 2004 round of negotiations. The authors included a number of new modelling assumptions, combined with an updated database that better reflected market access, domestic support and export restrictions that existed in 2004 – in particular the inclusion of applied bilateral tariffs, domestic support (OECD PSE) and changes to labour market assumptions. The former two developments have now been mainstreamed into the GTAP database (and so also included in METRO). Bouët et al. (2005) found that the gains from the implementation of the then proposed set of agricultural trade reforms were much lower than that found by other studies. In particular, for some developing countries the welfare effects of reform were either small or negative and trade levels increased much less than seen in other models. The results were driven by the low actual tariff cuts that formed part of the then potential agreement and preference erosion for some developing countries.

Tokarick (2008) provides a short summary of several CGE studies examining the welfare effects (measured as changes in real income) of agricultural trade liberalisation. This review, coupled with the author's own analysis highlighted:

- Tariff reform provides the greatest contribution to real income growth from agricultural trade liberalisation. This stems from relatively low use of subsidies (base years vary from 2001 to 1997), the economic effects of tariffs (subsidy plus consumption tax versus only subsidy) and the more extensive use of tariff protection for agricultural products.
- Benefits to flow to developing countries depend on both their agricultural trade status (net exporter or net importer) and, critically, on their own liberalisation efforts. Indeed Francois, van Meijl and van Tongeren (2005) find that own liberalisation is critical to the potential gains that may accrue to developing countries.
- While the benefits of own liberalisation vary for developing countries (from less than those conveyed from developed country reforms to significantly greater), in general, much of any

negative effect from developed country liberalisation can be offset by reforms to their own protection regimes.

- The critical importance in the estimated impacts of agricultural liberalisation are estimates made with respect to the degree of substitutability between domestic and international goods. The more homogenous, the greater the benefits (or lower the costs) imposed on developing countries from liberalisation.
- Across most studies, preference erosion for developing countries was not found to be a significant issue.

Anderson, Cockburn and Martin (2011) also provide a summary of results from agricultural trade reform based on results from the LINKAGE model. They also show that based on 2004 policy and trading patterns, developed countries were likely to gain more from trade reform than others, but that farm incomes in developing countries would rise, causing the farm non-farm wage gap to fall. A summary of the results from studies that linked the CGE modelling results to household level data highlighted that agricultural (and merchandise more general) trade reform had significant potential to reduce poverty and inequality in developing countries.

The OECD has also conducted its own modelling related to agricultural trade and domestic market reforms. A comprehensive report into international, national and household level effects was completed in 2006 (OECD, 2006). This study, using AGLINK and GTAPEM, found the economy-wide welfare gains were likely to be positive for the majority of individual countries and regions analysed. The magnitude of multi-sector reform benefits, when expressed as a percentage increment in GDP, is higher for the non-OECD region than the reform induced gain in welfare estimated for the OECD region. The household levels effects were found to be greatest for those households which supplied labour to commercial agricultural production. For other households, either diversified income sources or for subsistence households, limited market interaction, muted the impacts of agricultural trade reform.

Some studies have also explored the potential advantages of achieving agreement, even if the level of reform was modest. Bouët and Larborde (2009) suggest that without an agreement, a shift towards protectionism by countries increasing tariffs to bound rates would be costly in both trade and welfare terms. These costs could be significantly mitigated through the signing of even a modest agreement.

3.3 The impacts of current agricultural policies

In this section the impacts of agricultural trade and domestic support policies on agro-food markets, domestic economies and the global economy are explored. For some agricultural products, production is directly consumed and so is analogous to outputs from the food sector. Similarly, some products from the food sector are inputs into other production activities and so are also not final. While no perfect delineation between the categories is possible, for this study, agriculture is broadly defined as primary production activities with food as processing activities. Details are provided in Table A.2 (agriculture represents sectors 1-10 and food 11-19).

On production

A number of current trade barriers and domestic support policies are used with the intention of promoting agricultural production. Many, however, actually depress production. Agricultural production is estimated to be higher in a number of regions in the absence of current policy interventions, including in some countries that have relatively high levels of support, such as Europe and Indonesia (Figure 3.2, and more detailed information on production changes by sector and region is provided in Annex 3.A2). The reasons for this and the specific effects on production activities vary. They relate to both uneven levels of support and changes in world market prices that would occur if all countries moved away from their current set of production distorting policies.

For agricultural producers with low levels of protection such as Australia, New Zealand, Brazil and South Africa, policies used in other countries significantly impact on their production. For example, production would be around 10% higher in Australia if domestic support and trade distortions in other countries were removed.

However, for some countries, trade and domestic support policies do promote domestic production. In China, Japan, India, Mexico, the Russian Federation and the Middle East and North Africa (MENA) region, overall production levels fall when these policies are removed. For some, this is mainly due to the removal of policies that lead to higher domestic prices for targeted products and encourage domestic production (such as in Japan and Malaysia in the case of rice, Canada in the case of raw milk and the European Union in terms of sugar beet). For others it is both the removal of domestic support policies and changes in world prices that induce production falls (such as China and India). In countries in the MENA region, much of the production changes occur due to the effects on world prices.

Figure 3.2. Impacts of removal of current policies on agricultural and food production

% changes

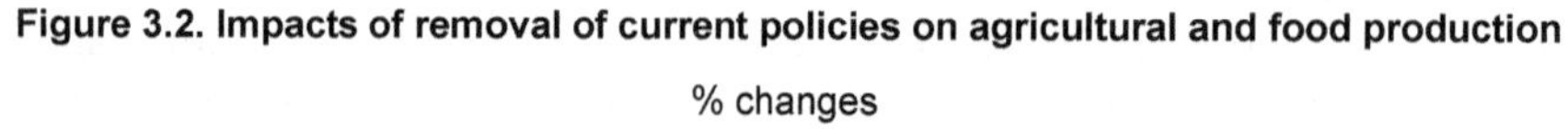

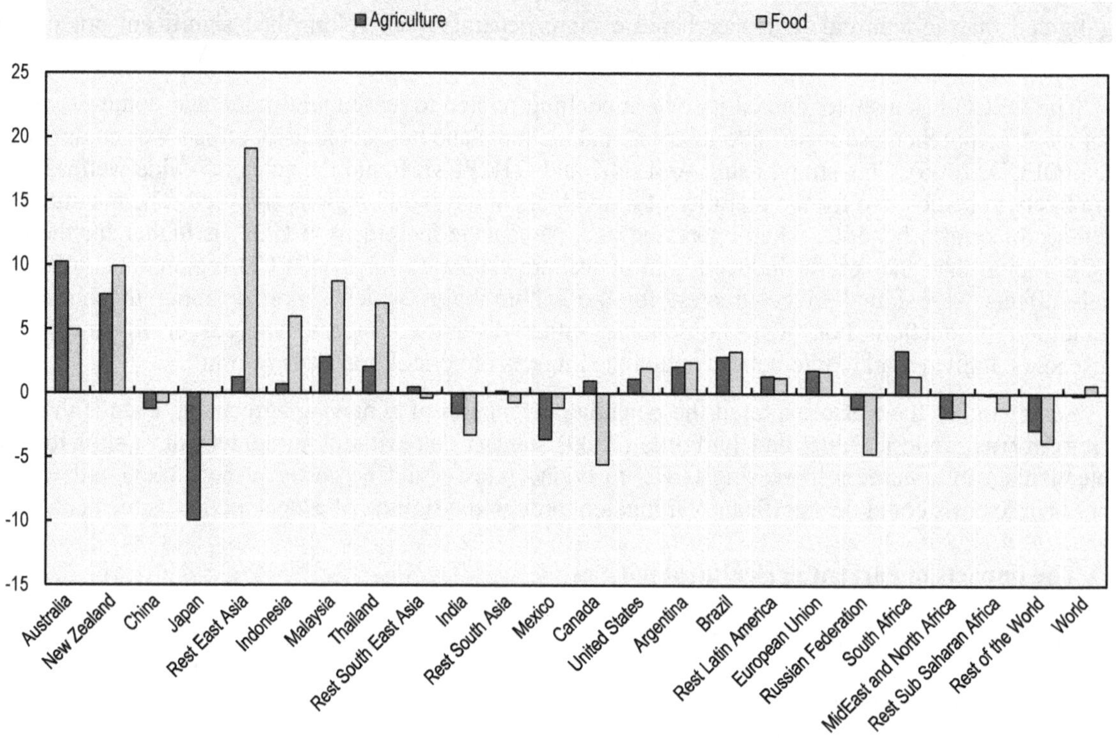

Source: Author estimates from METRO.

Overall, the total impacts of current policies on global production are estimated to be small. World production in agricultural products is marginally lower without current policies, but only by around 0.1%. This suggests that the main impact of current policies on world production is on the distribution of activities between countries and regions (as the country effects are relatively larger).

Changes in food production[3] generally mirror changes in agricultural production. Again, these changes are driven by a range of factors including tariffs imposed on food products, but also as a result of changes in the production of domestically produced agricultural products which are a major input into the food sectors. There are some exceptions. Food production in Canada falls by around 5% even though its agricultural production increases. This is mainly driven by a re-orientation of its agricultural sector. Current policies promote dairy which, if they were removed, would lead to a decrease in milk production (by around 36.7%). However, the removal of dairy policies, and changes in other countries' policies, encourage an expansion in wheat (46.1%) and fruit and vegetable production (11.7%). These products are mainly exported.

Interestingly, in terms of production expansion, overall food production without current agro-food trade and domestic support policies would be around 0.7% higher. The increase in food production given the marginal fall in world agricultural production is less contradictory than it seems. While being a main input, agricultural products only constitute a part of all inputs into food production (around 35%). Another 25% comes from production from the food industry itself, while the remaining inputs are provided by manufacturing and services, 15% and 25% respectively. In practical terms, this increased production may be in the form of a more productive food sector as it is able to use agricultural inputs more efficiently in reaction to changing prices and supplies.

The effects of policies differ across the different agricultural and food products examined (Figure 3.3). Global production decreases for rice, wheat, oil seeds, plant based fibres, other crops and wool, but production of other products increases. The biggest result, however, is observed in rice. Overall, world production of rice decreases by 2.1%, with a significant shift in production away from Japan to predominately Thailand and the United States (Annex 3.A2). Despite this, trade in rice increases (as discussed below). Wheat is another commodity where current policies lead to greater levels of production than might otherwise occur. Wheat production decreases mainly in MENA, India, United States and China and increases mainly in Canada, the Russian Federation, the Rest of the World region and the European Union. In aggregate, this creates a net decrease of around 0.8%. For animal production, the effects are both an increase in production and a re-allocation of activity. Increases are seen across countries in Oceania and most of the Americas (except Mexico and Canada).

Figure 3.3. Impacts of removal of current policies on world production, sectors

% changes

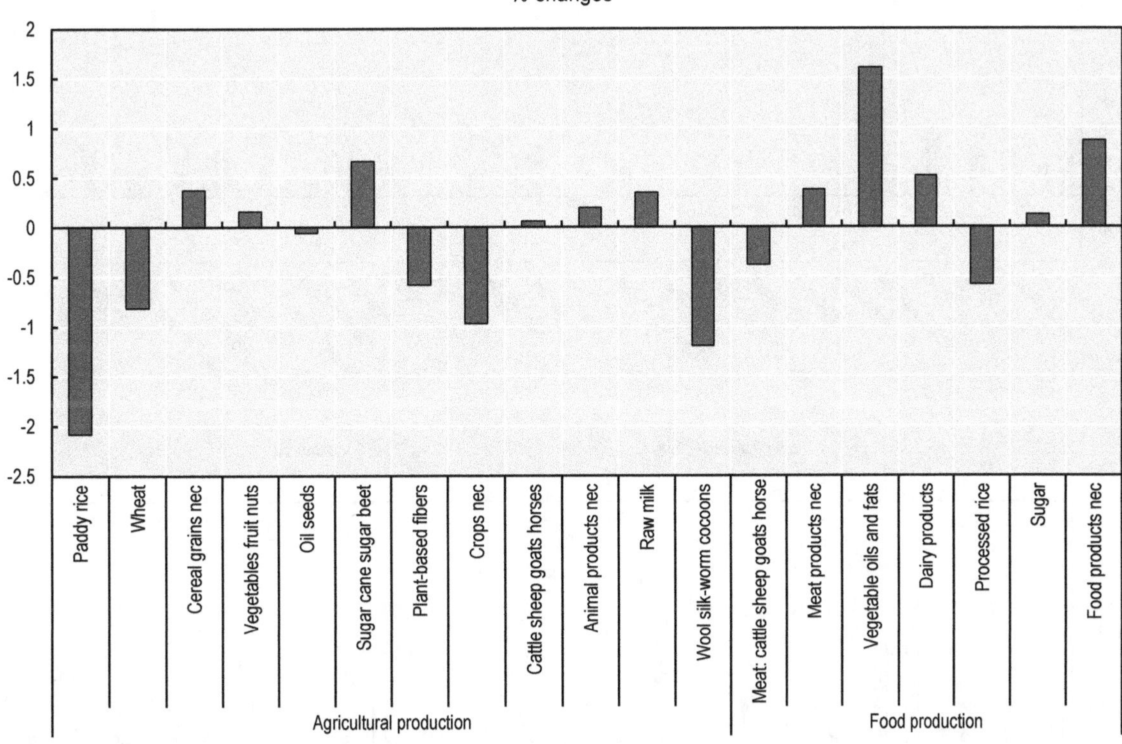

Source: Author estimates from METRO.

While only appearing as a moderate net effect, oil seed production experiences a considerable regional production shift (Annex 3.A2). Overall, world production falls marginally by 0.1%, but there is a significant decrease in production in China, Argentina and India, which is offset by higher production levels in Malaysia, Indonesia, Brazil, Rest of Latin America, the European Union and the United States. Similarly for wool, the removal of current policies creates a significant reallocation of activity. Decreasing production in China of around 41.3% is alleviated by strongly increasing production in Australia, 98.1% (net impact is a fall of 1.2%).

In regards to food sectors, global production of dairy products and vegetable oils and fats increase while the impacts of meat products are mixed (Figure 3.2). Again, for many of these sectors there is significant re-allocation of production activity across the globe (Annex 3.A2).

On trade

Current agricultural policies hinder overall agro-food trade. In the absence of the current suite of policies agricultural trade would be 5.3% higher and trade in food products would be 9.7% higher. Increasing food trade occurs for all regions, while the story for individual agricultural products is mixed (Figure 3.4).

Figure 3.4. Impacts of removal of current policies on trade in agro-food products by region

Agriculture Exports
Food Exports
70
60
50
40
30
20
10
0
-10
-20
Australia
New Zealand
China
Japan
Rest East Asia
Indonesia
Malaysia
Thailand
Rest South East Asia
India
Rest South Asia
Mexico
Canada
United States
Argentina
Brazil
Rest Latin America
European Union
Russian Federation
South Africa
MidEast and North Africa
Rest Sub Saharan Africa
Rest of the World
World

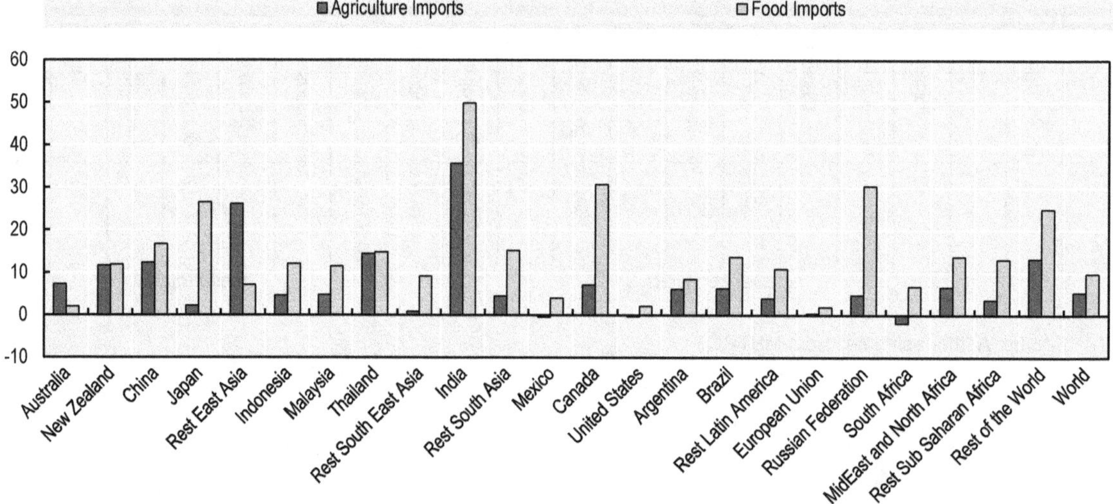

Source: Author estimates from METRO.

The effects vary across countries with many changes unrelated to changes in production. In Japan, for example, agricultural exports increase by around 21%, while agricultural production decreases by around 10% (on the back of falling rice production). These changes are brought about by shifts in the relative importance of different agricultural sectors in total production, along with changing prices for agricultural and food products. In New Zealand, the effects on trade are also distinct from production, but for different reasons. Increased agricultural production is consumed domestically by the even stronger increased food production. This is because agricultural exports constitute only a relative small share of New Zealand's total agro-food exports. Exports are dominated by the food sectors of meat and dairy which account for around 73% of total agro-food exports. Exports of these products increase by around 38.5% and 12.2% respectively.

Taking a closer look at Japan's trade and production changes reveals that the effects of current policies are complex. Removal of domestic support means that the cost of production increases. On the demand side, higher cost domestic produce must compete with relatively lower priced imports, leading to falls in demand and production. For food products, changes to policies cause domestic prices to fall. For the food industry, higher cost inputs from agriculture and lower output prices (as a result of more international competition) lead to decreasing food production, both for intermediate use and final consumption (Table 3.1). Demand for agricultural and food intermediates decreases accordingly (depicted by decreasing intermediates supply; Table 3.1, right columns). As a result of these effects, agricultural production further decreases, but there is also a reallocation to final consumption goods, which increase by 4.7%. However, the fall in the price of food products domestically increases the competitiveness of some of Japan's food exports globally. Given the relatively small export shares in overseas markets, the price effect creates a relatively larger increase in total exports (in percentage terms).

Increasing trade in most products (Figure 3.5) also suggests that trading patterns across the world are altered by current policy settings. Rice and wool are especially affected (both are traded predominately as intermediate products). For these products, current policies cause a large disruption to the location of production across regions and therefore trade. In other products, current policies also alter the location of processing. For example, trade of sugar beets and cane decreases while its global production increases. This occurs as more regions produce their own sugar rather than trade in the intermediate product in the absence of high barriers on the final consumption good (sugar). Production and trade in plant-based fibres also decreases, as a result of decreasing demand for this product once current policies are removed.

While exports in agricultural and food products show differing patterns in a number of countries, the story for imports is more uniform (Figure 3.6). Current agro-food policies generally limit imports of agro-food products for all countries, either directly through barriers to their importation, or indirectly by altering the costs of final products. Imports (and trade in general) in intermediate products is particularly limited by current policies. These patterns indicate that current policies are likely to be having significant negative effects on the participation in global value chains by producers in a number of countries.

Table 3.1. Linking production and trade in Japan's agro-food sectors

% Change	Production		Exports		Imports		Supply in Japan	
	Intermediate use	Final consumption	Intermediate use	Final consumption	Intermediate use	Final consumption	Intermediate use	Final consumption
Total	-9.77	-2.11	2.95	11.00	27.07	51.06	-4.88	2.72
Agriculture	-15.88	4.66	-2.21	31.37	25.41	2.81	-10.63	3.71
Food	-6.58	-2.81	5.80	6.90	28.36	58.96	-1.64	2.61

Source: Author estimates from METRO.

Figure 3.5. Impacts of removal of current policies on trade by commodity

% changes by end use categories

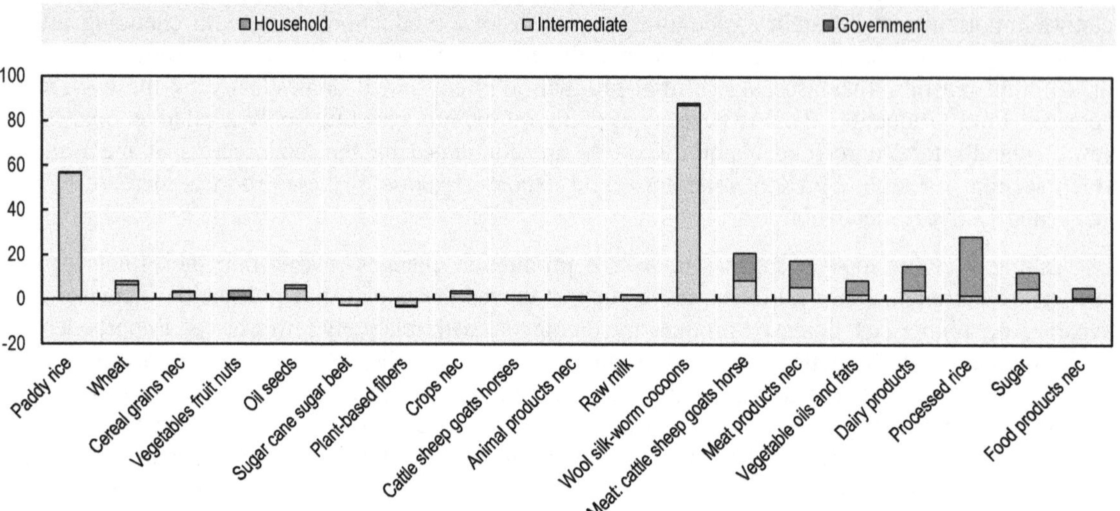

Source: Author estimates from METRO.

Figure 3.6. Impacts of removal of current policies on imports of intermediates by region

% changes

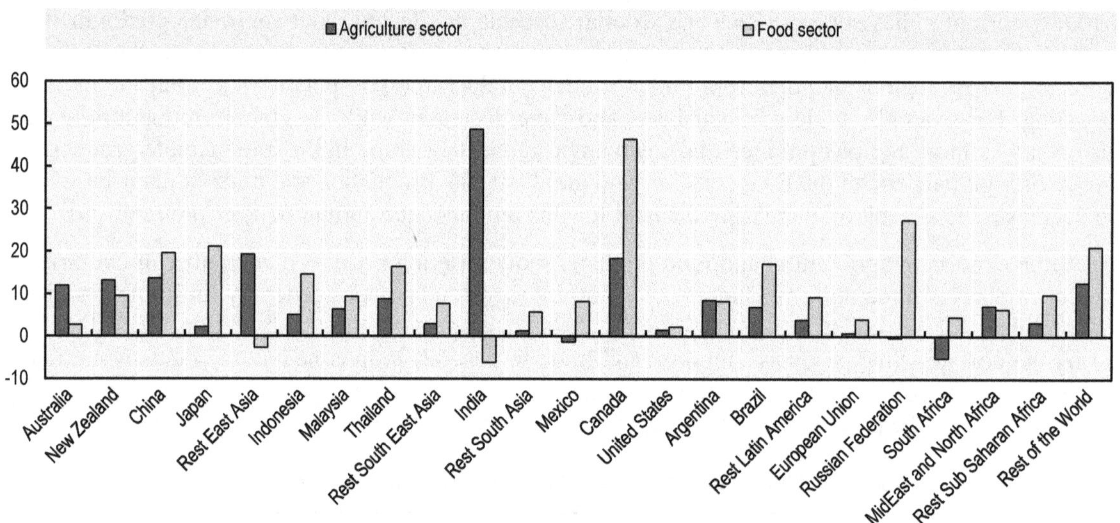

Source: Author estimates from METRO.

On consumption and total production

The effects of agro-food policies on the total economy are relatively small given that agro-food sector accounts for only a small part of total production in many countries. Despite this, it is still of value to look at the economy-wide welfare and production effects as a number of the effects of policies directed towards the agro-food sector occur outside the sector.

Total production, that is output from all sectors in the economy, is estimated to be higher in most regions if governments did not intervene in agricultural markets (Table 3.2). In some regions, production increases are driven by the agro-food sector itself, such as Australia and New Zealand. In other regions it is driven by a reallocation of resources away from agriculture to other sectors, such as in Japan. In the former group, where increases in agro-food sector production increase total production, the reallocation of resources to agro-food sectors causes a contraction in activity in non-agro-food sectors, but weaker than the positive impact on the agro-food sector. Total production decreases in China, India, Mexico, Canada and the Russian Federation. In these countries the growth effect in non-agro-food sector output is not strong enough to mitigate decreasing agricultural and food production.

Looking beyond agro-food sectors, the result of current agro-food policies on total trade is also negative. In the absence of such policies, all regions exhibit stronger engagement in trade: total exports and imports increase in all regions. There is one exception, that of Argentina, where exports decrease slightly due to falling manufacturing exports.

Changes in production do not, however, indicate the effects on welfare. Welfare can be proxied by changes in household incomes or consumption. While acknowledging that this is only partial, it provides a broader lens by which to assess changes than that of production or GDP. Private consumption represents the income that households receive from activities related to production as measured in the model. However, private household income is also dependent on other policy assumptions made in the model. Importantly, government policies related to taxation and government consumption will influence the levels of private income and therefore household welfare. In the base setting, it has been assumed that while governments maintain the *volume* of their consumption they vary the *value* of their consumption (and taxation) as a result of policy changes (flexible income tax). That is, if government expenditures fall, say through lower support payments or in reaction to changes in prices, then so does their tax. This implies that some of the savings from reform are shared with private households (and vice versa).[4] Alternatively, it could be assumed that tax rates remain fixed and governments maintain the value of their consumption. Taking the previous example, the savings from changes in domestic support or changes in prices are spent elsewhere by the government sector. An alternative way of thinking about the differences in the assumptions is that under the flexible income tax assumptions, governments provide some compensation or redistribution of any gains from policy reform (or conversely are compensated themselves by households). In the fixed income tax settings, governments (or households) do not.

Table 3.2. Impacts of removal of current policy on total production and trade

% change

	Australia	New Zealand	China	Japan	Rest East Asia	Indonesia	Malaysia	Thailand	Rest South East Asia	India	Rest South Asia	Mexico	Canada	United States	Argentina	Brazil	Rest Latin America	European Union	Russian Federation	South Africa	MidEast and North Africa	Rest Sub Saharan Africa	Rest of the World
Total imports	2.13	9.05	0.86	3.26	2.16	2.69	1.89	1.38	0.65	1.85	1.12	0.12	3.68	0.61	3.30	4.52	1.25	0.30	1.87	0.95	0.86	1.09	1.90
Total exports	1.03	2.54	0.81	2.13	1.60	1.80	1.01	0.67	0.48	1.22	2.35	0.28	1.83	0.16	-0.31	2.00	1.08	0.20	1.56	0.51	0.88	1.46	1.38
Total production	0.27	1.26	-0.07	0.15	1.15	0.11	0.62	0.31	0.05	-0.48	0.16	-0.07	-0.05	0.03	0.25	0.14	0.11	0.06	-0.17	0.11	0.00	0.01	0.03
Agriculture	10.21	7.69	-1.26	-9.97	1.23	0.68	2.81	2.04	0.48	-1.59	0.14	-3.59	0.97	1.12	2.08	2.85	1.35	1.80	-1.16	3.34	-1.80	-0.08	-2.82
Food	4.95	9.88	-0.79	-4.07	19.09	5.97	8.73	7.04	-0.39	-3.27	-0.72	-1.13	-5.54	1.94	2.39	3.24	1.23	1.72	-4.69	1.36	-1.74	-1.24	-3.81
Extraction	-1.15	-5.54	0.15	0.85	0.44	-0.81	-0.24	-0.35	-0.03	0.51	0.23	0.04	0.16	-0.25	-1.26	-1.74	-0.19	-0.13	0.56	-0.23	0.33	0.45	0.32
Manufacturing	-1.33	-5.46	0.17	1.18	1.05	-1.58	-0.64	-1.11	-0.13	0.05	0.81	0.37	0.60	-0.33	-1.47	-1.10	-0.25	-0.23	0.55	-0.33	0.53	0.73	1.21
Services	0.22	1.20	-0.02	0.07	0.13	0.13	0.17	0.23	0.12	-0.09	-0.02	0.04	0.02	0.06	0.37	0.18	-0.04	0.03	-0.14	0.11	-0.13	-0.07	0.02

Source: Author estimates from METRO.

The impacts on consumption under both flexible and fixed income tax closures are shown in Table 3.3.[5] In Table 3.3, another variable is shown which is termed 'absorption'. Absorption measures total demand (private, government and investment) for final goods in an economy. Absorption increases in all but five regions when agro-food policies are removed – those of China, Rest of South Asia, Mexico, MENA and Sub-Saharan Africa. Differences between the two closure assumptions show that under both, total demand remains relatively similar, but there are sometimes conflicting effects on households (and so household welfare). The difference is driven critically by how the effects of changes in current agro-food policies are shared, especially given the significant use of tariffs and subsidies that directly influence government income.

Decreasing tariff revenues in South Asia, MENA and Sub-Saharan Africa are the main determinants behind falling absorption in these regions (as can be seen in the fixed tax rate closure results in Table 3.3). And while households benefit from higher consumption due to lower prices and higher returns from endowments provided to other sectors of the economy, these benefits do not outweigh the falls in tariff revenues. In aggregate, however, the net effects are relatively small.

The changes in private consumption between the two closures indicate that for some countries, any gains from reform for households are reliant on some redistribution of the benefits (Table 3.3). For some countries, without redistribution, households would face falls in incomes (and thus consumption). This is the case in India and the United States. In these countries, domestic support is significant, and in the case of the United States, tariffs across a range of agricultural products are relatively low. In reverse, in a number of countries the government sector is made worse off from reforms due to lower revenues despite the economy as a whole benefiting.

The impacts of current policies also vary in their effects on labour income (Figure 3.7). In most countries, the effects on all types of labour income of agricultural policies are negative. This is due to the fact that current policies generally discourage labour employment by other sectors of the economy. However, it is not so in all countries. In China, India, Mexico and the United States, agricultural and other low skilled workers see wage falls if agricultural policies were removed. However, it should be noted that the agro-food sector also employs workers from across all employment categories, suggesting relative wages within the industry also change.

Table 3.3. Impacts of removal of current policy on consumption

% change

	Australia	New Zealand	China	Japan	Rest East Asia	Indonesia	Malaysia	Thailand	Rest South East Asia	India	Rest South Asia	Mexico	Canada	United States	Argentina	Brazil	Rest Latin America	European Union	Russian Federation	South Africa	Middle East and North Africa	Rest Sub Saharan Africa	Rest of the World
Flexible income tax - flexible government income																							
Absorption	0.22	1.91	-0.01	0.05	0.26	0.19	0.61	0.57	0.11	0.23	-0.07	-0.04	0.23	0.08	0.62	0.32	0.05	0.04	0.04	0.16	-0.09	-0.14	0.07
Government consumption	0.02	0.97	-0.05	-0.09	-0.96	0.06	-0.04	0.17	0.00	0.12	-0.25	0.09	0.00	0.05	0.30	0.19	-0.11	-0.02	-0.11	-0.01	-0.33	-0.45	-0.17
Private consumption	0.39	2.83	-0.01	0.12	0.69	0.33	1.08	0.94	0.17	0.37	-0.07	-0.08	0.42	0.11	0.87	0.46	0.10	0.08	0.12	0.27	-0.05	-0.13	0.16
Fix tax rates - predefined government income																							
Absorption	0.21	1.91	-0.04	0.05	0.25	0.20	0.57	0.55	0.10	0.22	-0.09	-0.05	0.23	0.09	0.61	0.31	0.05	0.04	0.04	0.16	-0.08	-0.14	0.07
Government consumption	0.43	1.92	3.54	0.02	-7.01	-0.91	-2.76	-3.09	-2.55	5.02	-4.79	1.92	0.04	0.71	0.81	0.54	-1.55	-0.14	-0.02	-0.24	-1.92	-4.17	0.08
Private consumption	0.25	2.51	-1.41	0.08	2.12	0.49	1.76	1.68	0.56	-0.59	0.47	-0.41	0.40	-0.04	0.75	0.33	0.41	0.13	0.08	0.35	0.44	0.58	0.09

Source: Author estimates from METRO.

Figure 3.7. Impacts of removal of current policy on endowment income

% changes

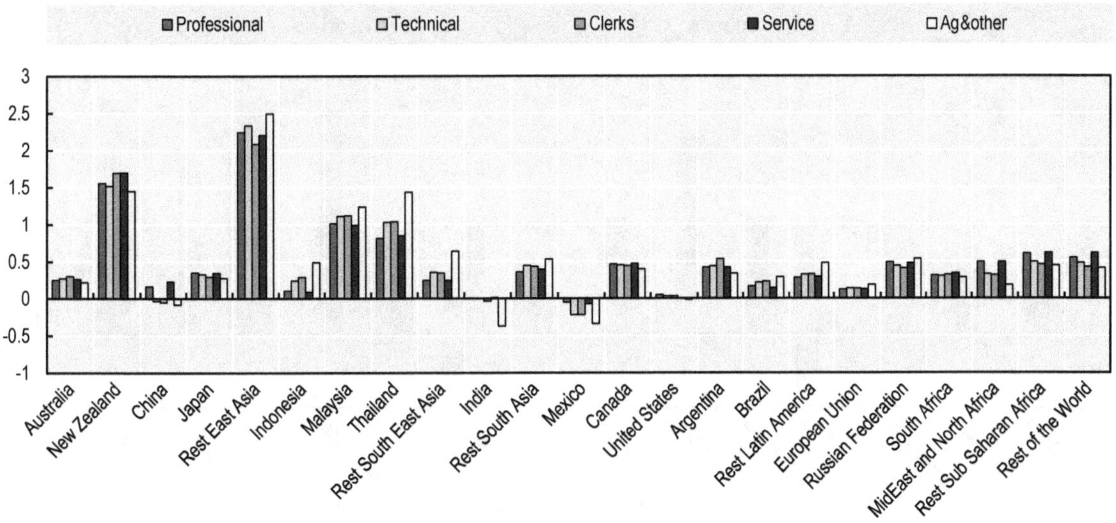

Professional | Technical | Clerks | Service | Ag&other

Australia, New Zealand, China, Japan, Rest East Asia, Indonesia, Malaysia, Thailand, Rest South East Asia, India, Rest South Asia, Mexico, Canada, United States, Argentina, Brazil, Rest Latin America, European Union, Russian Federation, South Africa, MidEast and North Africa, Rest Sub Saharan Africa, Rest of the World

Notes: Labour categories represent aggregated 2008 International Labour Organisation (ILO) Categories. Professionals includes ILO categories of Managers and Professionals (major groups 1 and 2); Technical includes ILO category Technical and Associate Professionals (major group 3); Clerks represents ILO category Clerical Support Workers (major group 4); Service represents ILO category Services and Sales Workers (major group 5); and Ag&other represents ILO categories Skilled Agricultural, Forestry and Fisheries Workers, Craft and Related Trades Workers, Plant and Machine Operators and Assemblers, and Elementary Occupations (major groups 6-9). See www.ilo.org/wcmsp5/groups/public/---dgreports/---dcomm/---publ/documents/publication/wcms_172572.pdf for more details.

Source: Author estimates from METRO.

Labour is not the only endowment factor affected by agricultural policies. Rents for land also change in most countries through the combination of the removal of land subsidies and changes in the returns to the agricultural sector (Figure 3.7). In the case of the United States, the major effects on household income result from changes in land rents rather than other effects. This is primarily due to the nature of the support offered to agricultural producers. For the four countries affected by wage decreases for agricultural and other low skilled workers, and the United States with respect to land, governments benefit from the policy change (indicated by increasing government consumption in Table 3.3). However, the differences in the closure assumptions in Table 3.3 show that the governments could alleviate the negative effects for households by transferring parts of the income increase to households (the net result for China is approximately neutral, that is, absorption effects are approximately zero).

3.4 A closer look at the effects on markets

It is worth exploring in more detail how the current suite of policy measures may affect the outlook for agricultural markets. In particular, what are the expected outcomes in terms of prices and trade flows over the medium term if such policies were not in place? The OECD-FAO AGLINK-COSIMO model provides a platform for assessing the likely effects on world agricultural markets. Estimates of these effects can be calculated using the current set of projections from the *Agricultural Outlook 2015* (OECD-FAO, 2015).

Prices

The measured trade and domestic support policies influence world prices, but on balance, that influence is relatively small. Further, interactions between different policy measures suggest that the price effects of policy interventions across all products are not all in the same directions (Figure 3.8).

Figure 3.8. Impacts of policy removal on trade flows and world prices

Selected commodities, difference to 2024 baseline

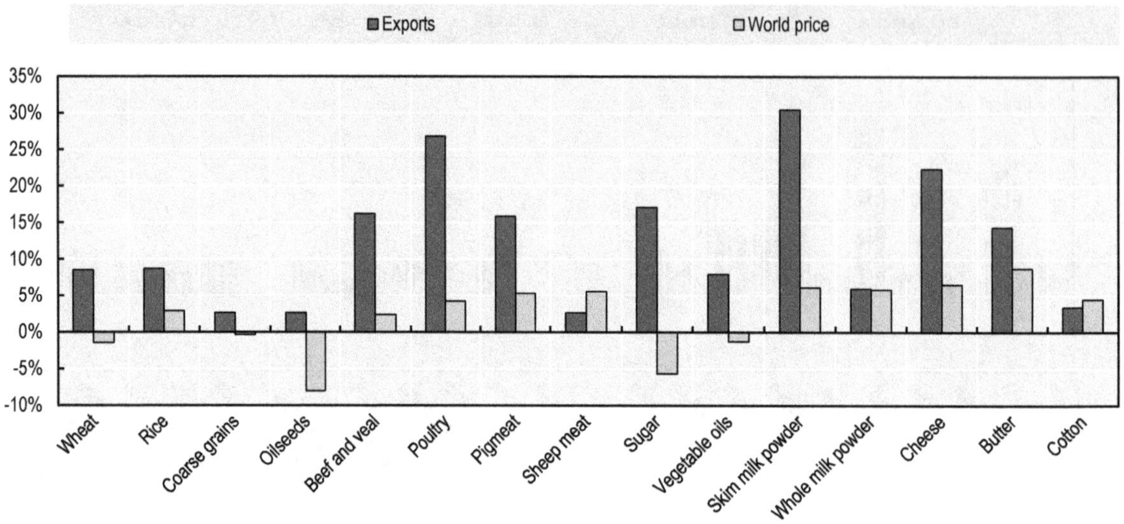

Notes: Sugar price refers to the United States domestic sugar price.

Source: Author estimates from AGLINK-COSIMO.

In general, agro-food trade and domestic support policies depress world prices. Prices for most agricultural products are expected to be higher in the absence of such measures. However, there are some exceptions. The results from the AGLINK-COSIMO simulations suggest that, in particular, the export taxes on oilseeds (soybeans) from Argentina inflate world prices. The removal of these export taxes subsequently leads to price falls. This has a flow-on effect on the price of vegetable oils where, due to the effects of other policy interventions, prices would also be expected to be lower in the absence of policy interventions.

In grains markets, the price effects of policies are relatively small. For rice, the limited price effect is likely a result of the range of measures simulated. For example, in Indonesia and a number of other rice-importing countries in Asia (such as the Philippines and Malaysia), trade distortions are mainly a result of import licensing arrangements, rather than the MFN tariffs. Because import licensing arrangements are not captured in the MFN tariff, they are not modelled in AGLINK-COSIMO (although they are included to some extent in METRO through *ad valorem* equivalents within the GTAP database). In wheat markets the effects are more complex. Overall, policies inflate world market prices through tariffs on animal products and biofuels which influence demand for wheat for feed in the Russian Federation and biofuels in the European Union.

For sugar, the price shown on Figure 3.9 is the United States domestic price. The impact of current policies inflates the United States domestic price (no world price for sugar exist in the model). For major sugar exporters, however, the price effects in domestic markets are limited with little change in prices created by current policies. The exception to this is Argentina, where in the absence of current policies domestic prices are estimated to rise. In other domestic markets across the world, domestic sugar prices are in general expected to fall in the absence of current policies (Figure 3.9).

World meat and dairy market prices are lower as a result of current policy interventions. These markets are primarily affected by the traditional tariff and quota type trade restrictions that dampen trade flows and as such world prices.

Figure 3.9. Impacts of policy removal on sugar prices

Difference to 2024 baseline, %

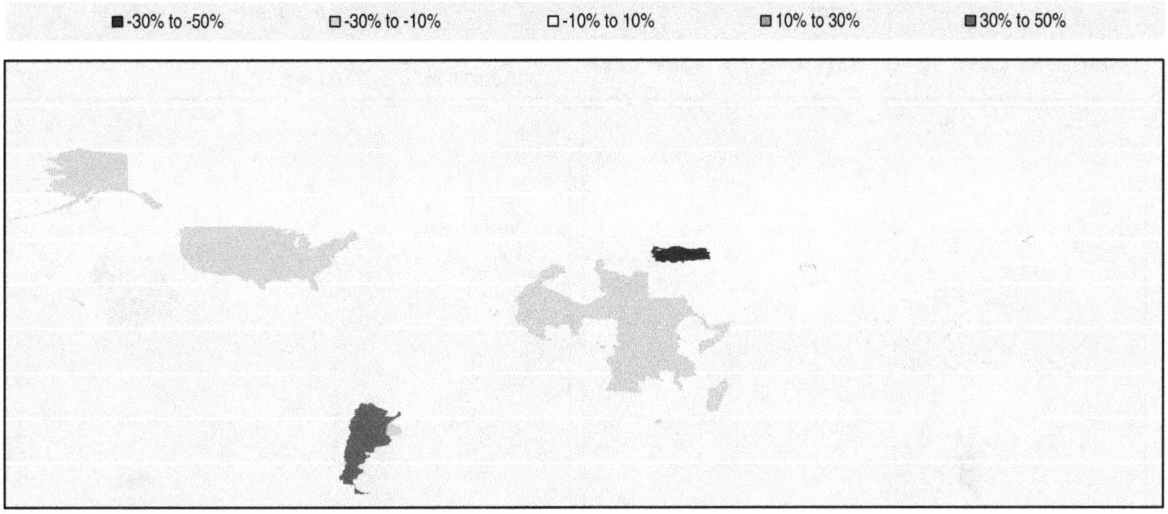

■ -30% to -50% □ -30% to -10% □ -10% to 10% ■ 10% to 30% ■ 30% to 50%

Source: Author estimates from AGLINK-COSIMO.

Trade flows

Current policy settings have the largest impact on trade flows in meat and dairy markets – this is in line with the observed price effects of current policies (which are greatest in meat and dairy markets, see Figure 3.8). Trade flows for a number of these products are considerably lower than what may otherwise occur. Given that demand for these products is projected to rise in the future, the efficiency cost of current policies, if maintained, is also expected to increase.

What is noticeable from expected effects on trade flows is that for all products examined, the impact of current policies is to restrict trade (as seen in the METRO model results). As a result, shares of production traded are lower than would otherwise be the case, making international markets in some products relatively thin. It is possible that the removal of such policies could both enhance trade flows and potentially increase confidence in international markets as with higher trading, the price effects in one region would be expected to be hedged to a greater extent by supplies from other regions.

The distribution of impacts on trade flows varies across products. Expected changes in trade volumes for oilseeds, beef and veal, and poultry are shown in Figures 3.10, 3.11 and 3.12.

For all the three products highlighted, much of the impact of current policy settings is felt by exporting regions in South America, in particular, Brazil and Argentina. For both oilseeds and poultry, changes in exports show an increase in total traded volumes as well as a shift in the relative importance of countries. For oilseeds, Argentina's export tax arrangements have led to greater trade flows from Brazil and the United States. For poultry, the trade effects of current policies are a combination of effects that relate to both direct trade policies along with indirect effects from changes brought about in relative feed costs. The impact of the removal of these policies on poultry trade is shown on Figure 3.11.

Figure 3.10. Impacts of policy removal on oilseed trade

Difference to baseline in 2024, kt

Exports
-25 to -15 Mt
-15 to -5 Mt
-5 to 5 Mt
5 to 15 Mt
15 Mt to 25Mt
Imports
-2.5 to -1.5 Mt
-1.5 to -0.5 Mt
-0.5 to 0.5 Mt
0.5 to 1.0 Mt
1 Mt to 1.5 Mt

Source: Author estimates from AGLINK-COSIMO.

Figure 3.11. Impacts of policy removal on beef and veal trade

Difference to baseline in 2024, kt

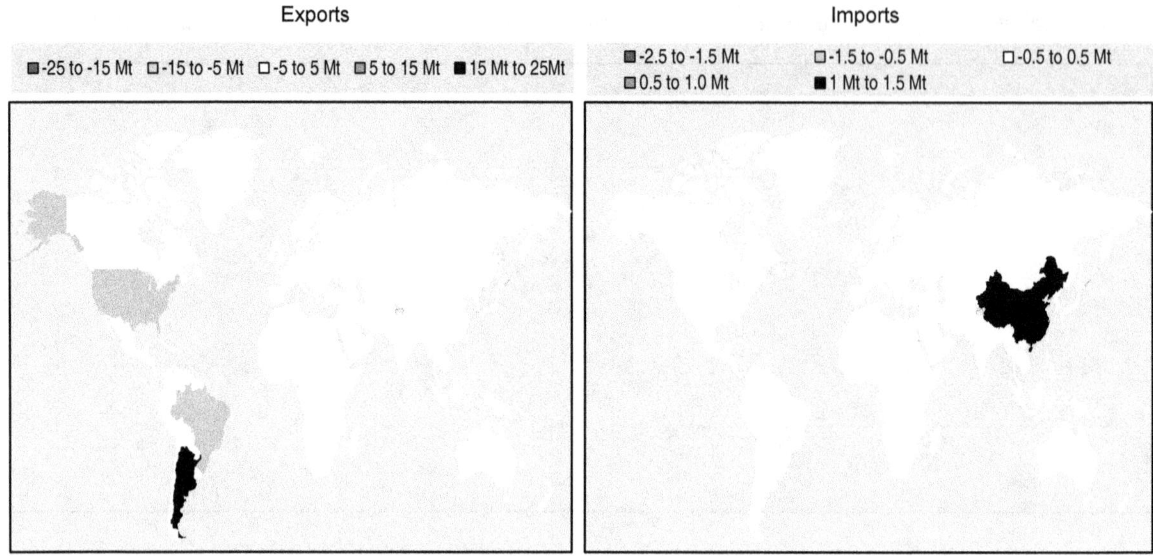

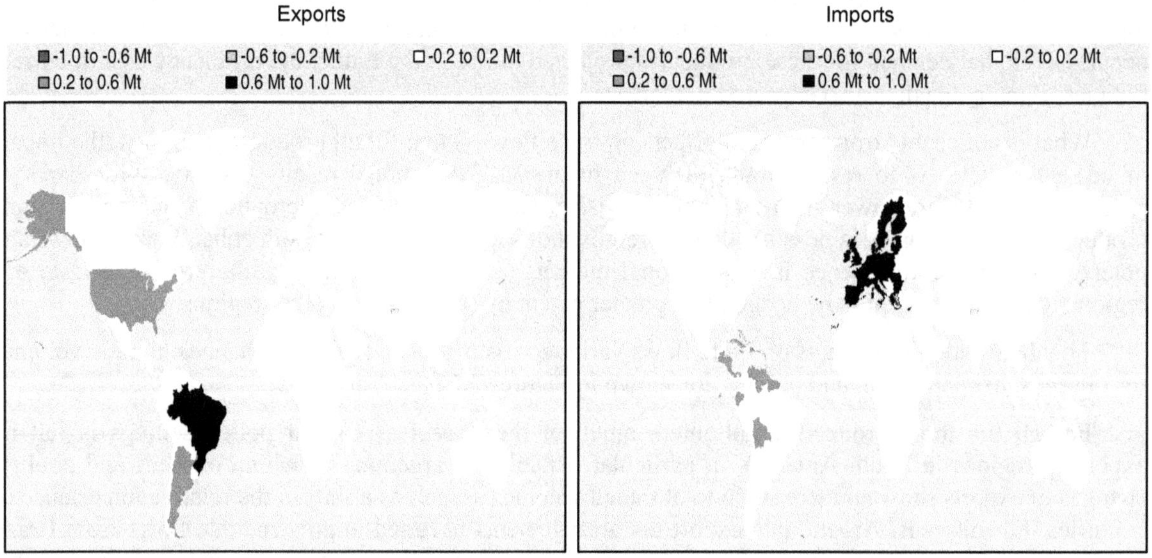

Exports
-1.0 to -0.6 Mt
-0.6 to -0.2 Mt
-0.2 to 0.2 Mt
0.2 to 0.6 Mt
0.6 Mt to 1.0 Mt
Imports
-1.0 to -0.6 Mt
-0.6 to -0.2 Mt
-0.2 to 0.2 Mt
0.2 to 0.6 Mt
0.6 Mt to 1.0 Mt

Source: Author estimates from AGLINK-COSIMO.

Figure 3.12. Impacts of policy removal on poultry trade

Difference to baseline in 2024, kt

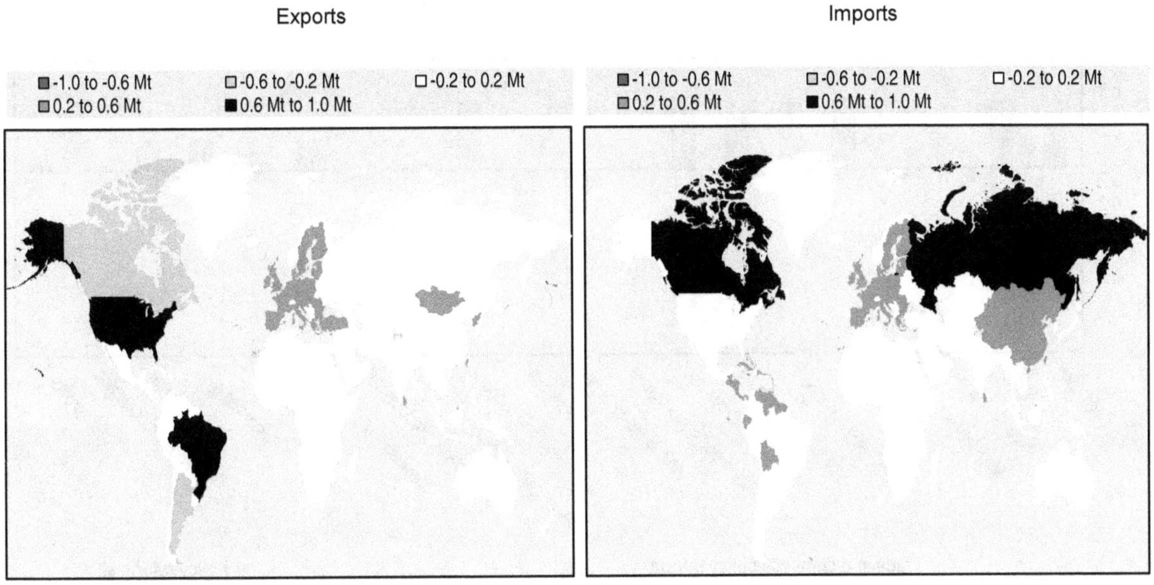

Exports

-1.0 to -0.6 Mt; -0.6 to -0.2 Mt; -0.2 to 0.2 Mt; 0.2 to 0.6 Mt; 0.6 Mt to 1.0 Mt

Imports

-1.0 to -0.6 Mt; -0.6 to -0.2 Mt; -0.2 to 0.2 Mt; 0.2 to 0.6 Mt; 0.6 Mt to 1.0 Mt

Source: Author estimates from AGLINK-COSIMO.

3.5 Impacts of possible multilateral reform scenarios

Looking beyond the impacts of the current set of policies, it is worth examining what are the possible impacts of trade reform on agriculture and food sectors. To do so, three scenarios are explored. First, a multilateral commitment to reform that sees modest changes in developed countries and only small changes in developing countries (*trade and domestic policy reform scenario,* for details see Section 3.2). Second, a situation where the multilateral agreement scenario is extended to developing countries and covers liberalisation efforts like those in developed countries (an extension of *trade and domestic policy reform scenario* termed *policy reform all* – for details see Section 3.2). Third a situation of no agreement compared with an agreement that locks in current levels of market access and domestic support. The latter so called *policy drift scenario* (for details see Section 3.2) shows the effects of stylised recent developments in agricultural markets over the period between 2011 and 2014. For all scenarios, the aggregate effects on the level of world agricultural and food production are only minor (Figure 3.13). However, it is found that increasing protection in some countries has the potential to affect all other regions negatively.

Under the *policy drift scenario* the effects vary across commodities, with crop production general increasing and livestock production falling (Figure 3.13). Across countries, both Malaysia and Indonesia experience production decreases, despite providing greater levels of support to the agricultural sector (but re-enforcing the current non-uniform targeting of individual production activities) (Figure 3.14). For these countries, the small increases in rice and crop production as a result of increased domestic support are not enough to overcome decreasing production of oil seeds and vegetable oils and fats (Annex 3.A2). That is, increased support causes a substitution away from productive to less productive agricultural sectors.

Conversely, production increases in China, India and the Russian Federation. In China, production increases are concentrated in oil seeds, wool and vegetable oils and fats. The reallocation of resources means that production of livestock, meat and milk decreases. This is also the main driver of increasing production in the Russian Federation.

Figure 3.13. Effects of trade reform on production, by sector

% change

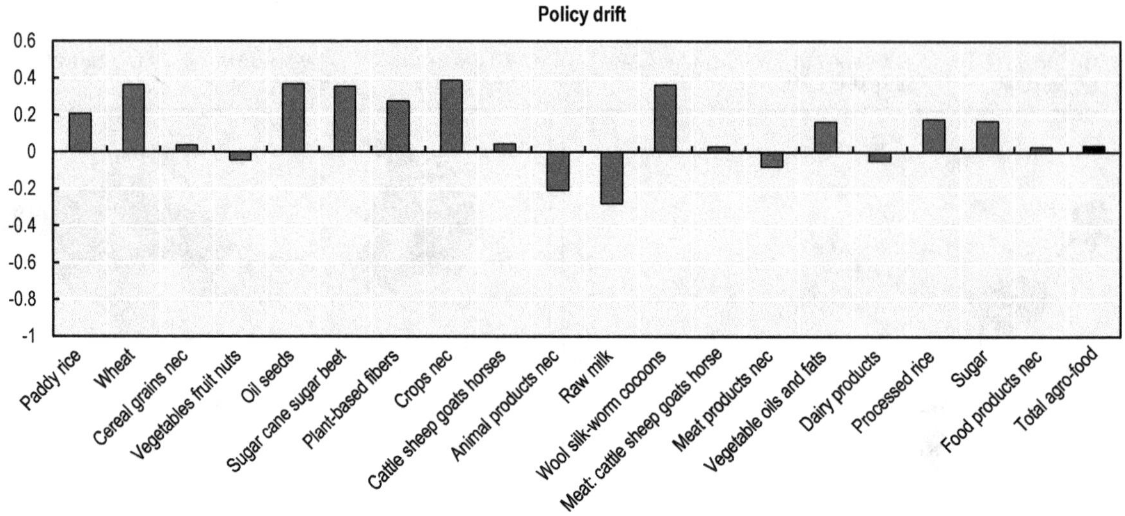

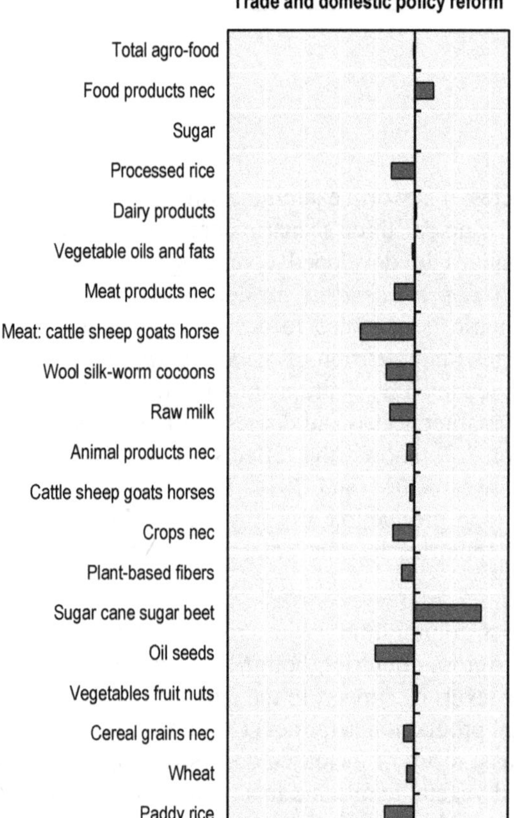

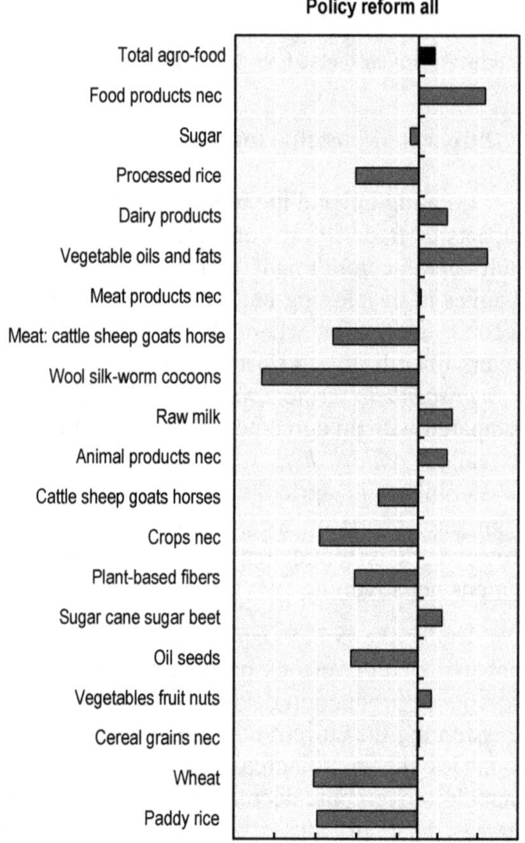

Source: Author estimates from METRO.

Effects on agro-food production in all other regions are small and negative, with the changes in production in China and India dominating the worldwide effects (Annex 3.A2). The largest effects are on agricultural production in Australia, Canada and Brazil which decrease more than 0.4%. These decreases occur mostly for wool (Australia) and oil seed production (Canada and Brazil), activities which both increase considerably in China. Food production increases in Argentina (and ROW aggregate region) as a result of increasing exports of vegetable oils and fats to India (Argentina has preferential access over other major exporters).

Under the *trade and domestic policy reform scenario* the net effects on production at the sector level are small, but agro-food production declines in a number of sectors (Figure 3.13). The uneven reform and remaining support create a situation where, despite some reform, production falls (albeit by a very small amount). This points to the benefits from greater coverage and depth of reform across all countries and, indeed, world agro-food production increases slightly (0.1%) when also developing countries join the multilateral agreement (Figure 3.13). However, effects vary across products and regions (Figure 3.14).

Figure 3.14. Effects of policy scenarios on production by country

% change

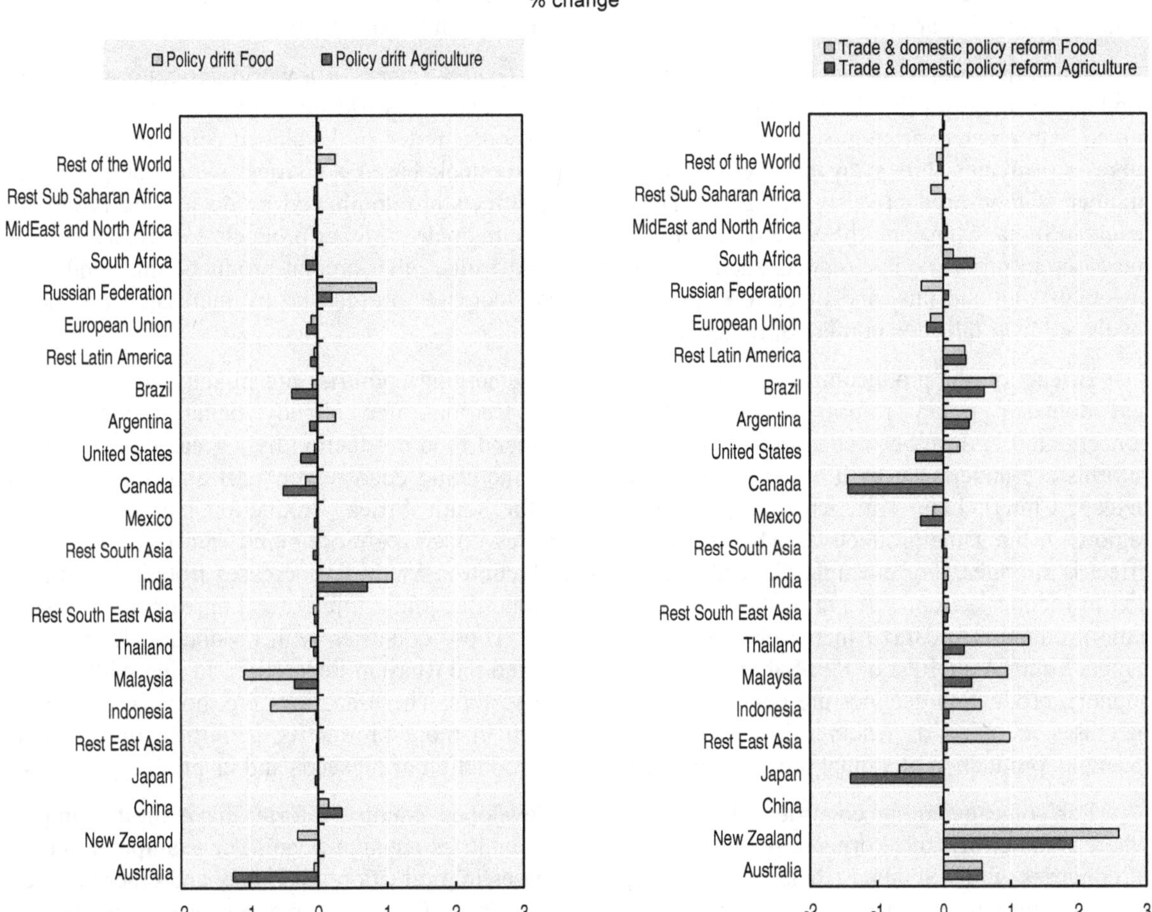

Source: Author estimates from METRO.

While the effects of *trade and domestic policy reform* on aggregate production are small, there are some significant changes in the distribution of production. Agricultural and food production increases in Oceania, East and Southeast Asia except for Japan, where production decreases, and China, which, like South Asia, does not show net effects on production (Figure 3.14). Production increases slightly in South Africa and South America, while production decreases of Mexico, Canada and the United States. Production declines are also expected in the European Union as a result of falling trade barriers. For other regions in Africa there are only small effects. This results occurs as countries in the region and their major trading partners are relatively unaffected by the reforms.

In terms of products, the changes in the *trade and domestic policy reform* scenario cause some shifts in where production is centred (Annex 3.A2). Wheat production shifts from the United States (decreases by 7.8%), to Canada and the Russian Federation (increases of 8.7% and 3.8% respectively). Oil seed production decreases in China (2.0%), Argentina (1.6%) and the United States (0.8%) and increases in smaller amounts in various regions around the world. Australia and New Zealand experience the largest increase of agro-food production. Both countries increase cattle and meat production (together with Latin America and Sub-Saharan Africa). These increases in cattle and meat production compensate for other decreases that occur mainly in the European Union. The European Union sees increasing production of milk and dairy. Sugar production shifts mainly from the European Union to Brazil.

When the reform also includes developing countries (*policy reform all*), world agricultural and food production increases (by 0.1%, Figures 3.14 and 3.15). Effects on world net production by product are mixed with greater variation seen than when reforms are concentrated in developed countries. In general, there is a greater shift away from crop production to livestock based activities, with production of a number of food products also increasing. The observed effects are dominated by decreasing production levels in India, China and the MENA region (Figure 3.15). In contrast, other products experience stronger increases in production – products such as vegetables and fruits, other animal products, milk and dairy, vegetable oils and fats, and other food products. These increases are caused by increasing production levels or lower falls in a number of regions.

Effects on the production levels of developing and emerging countries are mixed under both trade and domestic policy reform scenarios (Figure 3.15). Regions that already benefit from reforms concentrated in developed countries increase agricultural and food production by a greater amount when reforms are undertaken by a wider group of countries – including countries in East and Southeast Asia (except China); Latin America (except Mexico); and for South Africa. Production increases in these regions in the same products as when developed countries undertake more significant reforms, but the effect is stronger.[6] For example oil seed (palm oil) production in Malaysia increases from 1.3% to 5.0% and in Indonesia from 1.7% to 6.6% when developing countries join a multilateral agreement; and sugar cane production in Brazil increases from 1.4% to 2.5%. Those countries with production falls include China, South Asia, Rest of Sub-Saharan Africa, Mexico and the Russian Federation. In line with areas of support, production declines are concentrated in certain sectors. These declines are, however, offset but increases in others as resources are freed up to be used in more productive activities, In China, for example, production of animal products increases while production of oil seeds and its products decrease.

For some emerging countries, the effects from developed country reforms have limited impacts whereas the effects of reforms to policies in developing countries are significant. For example, a number of countries within Southeast Asia see much larger increases in production when they and other middle to low income countries participate in multilateral reform efforts. India also experiences greater changes with production declines seen across a number of sectors.

A number of developed countries see increases in production from a greater global coverage of reform efforts. The largest production effects are seen in Australia and New Zealand, particularly for animal production and products. Net production changes from negative to positive in Canada and the United States for agriculture, and for agriculture and food production in the European Union. This increasing net production is driven by increasing wheat production in Canada; and oil seeds, other crops, vegetables and fruits, and animal production in the United States. The European Union increases production of various products, while milk and dairy, meat (not cattle) and other food products dominate the positive net effect.

Across the three scenarios explored there are some interesting differences in production worth contrasting. At the global level, the results of trade and domestic policy reforms that see efforts concentrated in developed countries produce an on balance effect of virtually no change in net agro-food production. In contrast, some concentrated increases in support and protection to agriculture by some regions see an increase in production, driven predominately from impacts seen in China and India, albeit with significant efficiency costs (discussed below). However, a more global effort to remove distortions to agro-food markets yields the largest positive production response.

Figure 3.15. Contrasting liberalisation reforms

% changes

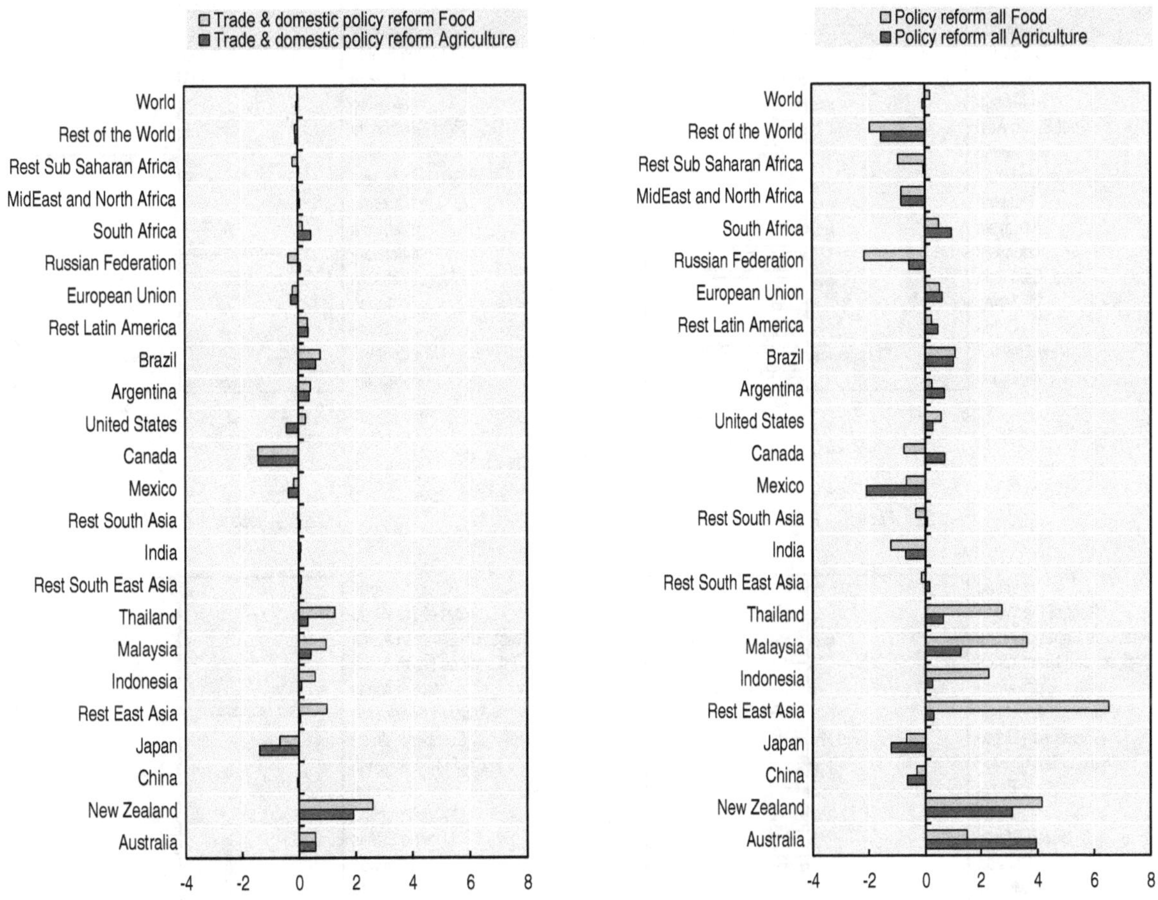

Source: Author estimates from METRO.

Trade

Under the *policy drift* scenario, the increasing levels of protection decrease trade in agro-food products (Figure 3.16). Agro-food imports decrease strongly, most notably in the regions with increasing protection (by up to 6%). Under this scenario, the effects on trade are concentrated in sectors that see the largest increases in protection. Countries increasing protection decrease their imports of these products, with effects on exports being distributed worldwide. Importantly, the effects of increases in protection in a few countries generally decrease exports for most regions. Exceptions to this are seen for agricultural exports from India, New Zealand, China and Malaysia, and food exports of Argentina (related to lower tariffs applied on vegetable oil products to India).

Figure 3.16. Impacts of trade and domestic policy reform and policy drift on trade

Trade reform | Policy drift

Exports (% changes)

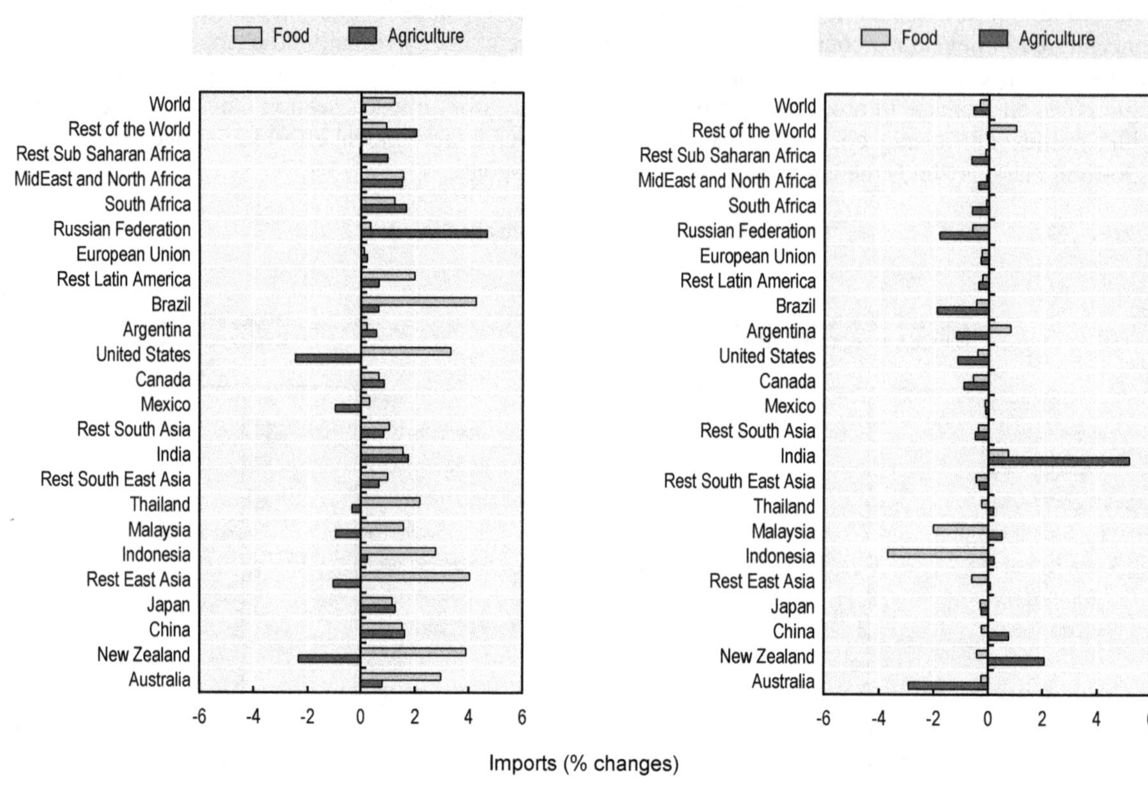

Imports (% changes)

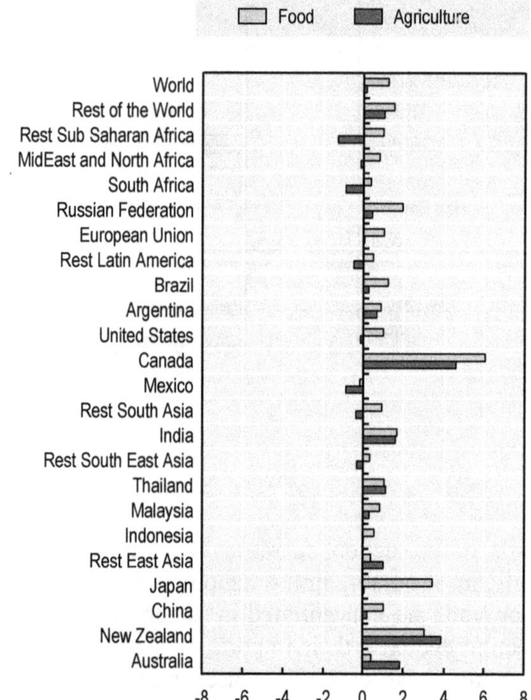

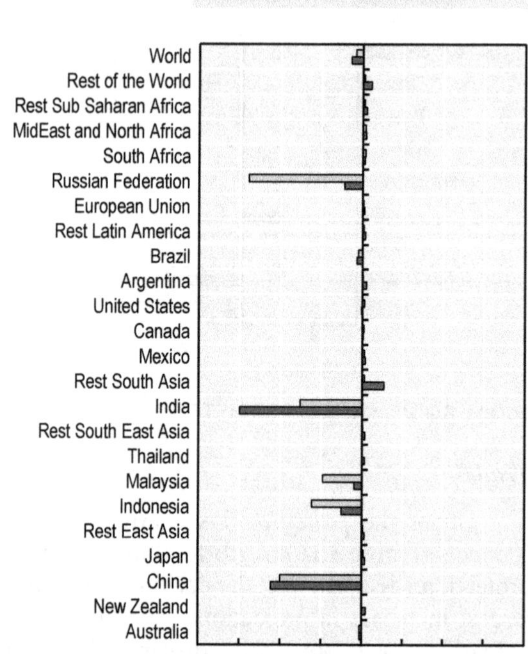

Source: Author estimates from METRO.

Figure 3.17. Impacts of trade and domestic policy reforms trade by use category

% changes

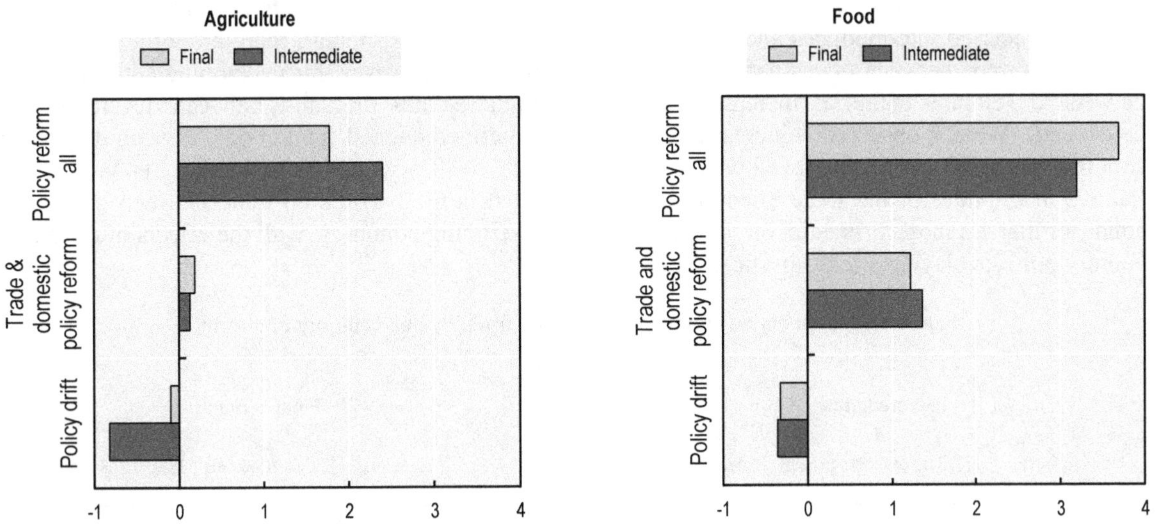

Source: Author estimates from METRO.

Reforms of the like described in the *trade and domestic policy reform* scenario, on the other hand, would increase trade. Agro-food exports and imports increase under this scenario in most regions. Total agro-food trade increases worldwide by just under 1%. In some countries the effects of reform differ across agricultural and food sectors, with some regions such as the United States and Mexico showing contractions in trade (and production) of agricultural products but see increases in trade (and production) of food products. In general, reforms move world production and trade towards levels that would be seen if policies were not in place (as described in Section 3.3) – the effects are just smaller.

When reforms are more widespread and analogous reforms take place across all countries (the *policy reform all* scenario), the effects are significantly larger. Total agro-food trade increases by 3% reflecting the wider coverage of reforms. For agricultural products, world trade increases by 2.1% from 0.1% and food increases by 3.5% from 1.2% compared with the *trade and domestic reform* scenario.

The results indicate that reforming agricultural markets would spur trade in intermediates to a greater extent that final goods. In both agricultural and food products, the changes in policies that take place within both the trade and domestic policy reform scenarios lead to larger increases in intermediates trade (Figure 3.17). In particular, for agricultural products, when developing countries reform their agro-food policies there is a significant increase in intermediate trade. This has implications for the development and participation in value chains by developing countries. It suggests that the policies that are currently in use are hampering developing countries participation in agro-food value chains and thereby limiting the potential gains available to agro-food sectors in these countries to exploit the potential benefits from GVCs.

Between the reform scenarios the effects on developed and developing countries differ. The main driver of the differences observed between the scenarios relate to the growing importance of so called 'south-south' trade. When reforms are concentrated in developed countries (*trade and domestic policy reform*), the trade effects on products sourced from developed countries are strongest for final goods. This scenario sees increased trade in final goods between developed countries and between developed countries and developing (Figure 3.18). In terms of intermediates, there is a substitution away from developed country products to developing. Developing countries on the other hand see more significant changes, with the effects on final good strongest (in line with generally higher rates of protection for final goods than intermediates). Exports to developed countries increase over 2%, considerably stronger than the trade effects between developed countries. South-south trade in intermediate and final goods also increases, but to a lesser extent.

When reform efforts are more widespread (*policy reform all*) the effects are both larger and the relative effects on intermediates and final goods trade change. In particular, there are large increases in final goods trade between developed and developing countries. However, for developing countries, trade between developing countries increases significantly (and remains the same between developing and developed). What is observed is increased trade in both intermediate and final goods between developing countries suggesting that the development of 'south-south' GVCs would be particularly enhanced. The relative magnitudes of the trade effects also suggest that it is the barriers on trade between developing countries that are most influential on the outcomes for developing countries, with the effects of developed country policies playing a less significant role.

Figure 3.18. Impacts on agricultural and food trade by use category of reform

% changes

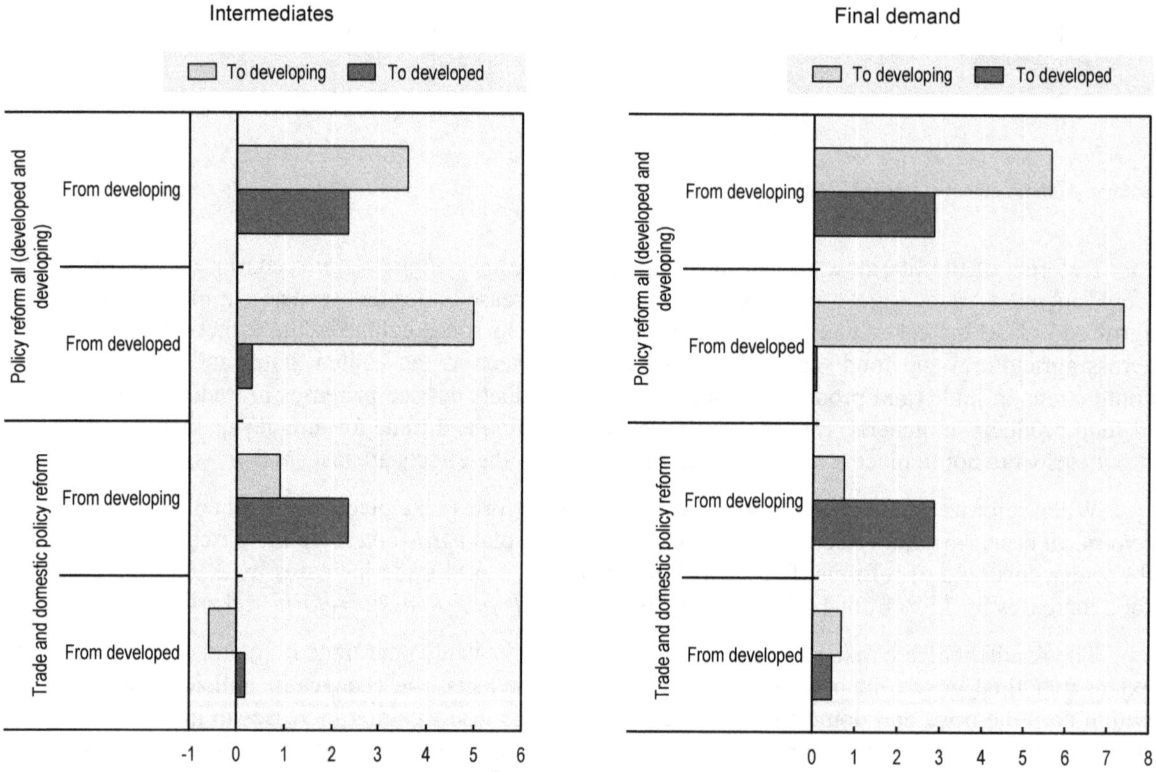

Source: Author estimates from METRO.

Under the more inclusive reform scenario (*policy reform all*) the effects on trade volumes for all countries are more significant as expected (Figure 3.19). However, changes in trade volumes also point to a number of interesting dynamics for individual countries. For India, for example, while production and exports of agricultural products decrease, exports of food products increase. This increase is driven by the lower price of intermediate inputs (sourced both locally and from imports) that result from the reforms. This creates an environment where the food processing sectors in India can become more internationally competitive, leading to increases in their exports. Changes like these help underpin the ultimate effects on economic activity and as such the benefits that are created from less distorted agricultural markets.

Figure 3.19. Impacts of developed and developing country reforms on trade

% changes

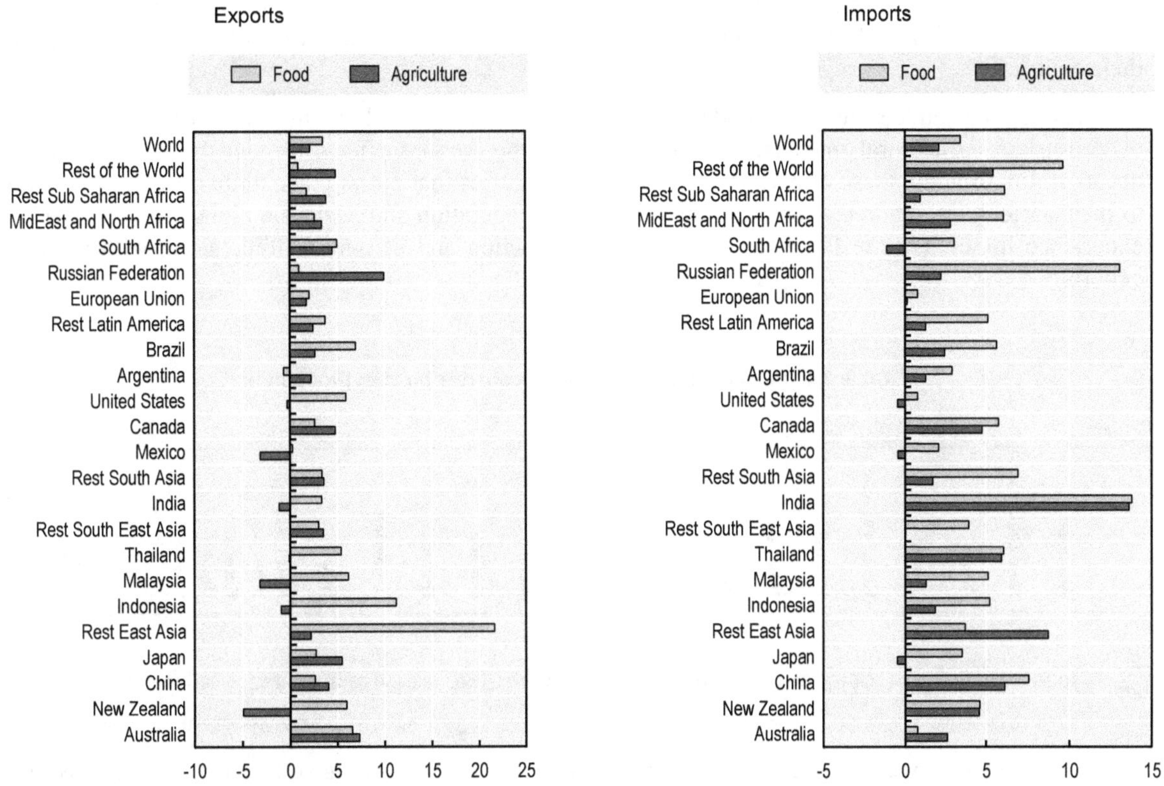

Source: Author estimates from METRO.

Private consumption and economic activity

Both the two trade and domestic policy reform scenarios and the policy drift scenario have a very small effect on the rest of the economy (Table 3.4). In aggregate, despite the sector specific impacts, there are only small changes in total production (across all commodities) in most economies. The largest production increases are seen in New Zealand (0.3%). Changes in aggregate imports and exports are dominated by the effects on agro-food trade. Effects are stronger when the trade reform includes developing countries, total imports and exports increase in all regions, except exports in Argentina which decrease slightly, 0.14%. Total production increases in most regions, with the largest increases in New Zealand, Rest of East Asia, Malaysia and Thailand. Total production decreases in the Russia Federation and India, while other regions do not show significant effects.

That said, for the countries that impose higher levels of protection on their agro-food sectors (*policy drift* scenario) the overall effects are generally negative. Indonesia is worst affected under the policy drift scenario with total production, total exports and total imports falling. This is due to both effects from their own policy decisions but also from those of others.

Trade reforms generally would have small but positive effects on private consumption, with larger effects seen under a scenario of more widespread reform efforts. Overall, New Zealand and Argentina see largest increases in private consumption – with Malaysia also experiencing larger gains if reforms were more widespread (Table 3.5). However, as noted above, variations between the winners and losses within countries mean that any transition needs to be carefully managed with the use of appropriate flanking policies such as social protection that allow for some redistribution of the possible gains. Flanking policies in some regions, such as Sub-Saharan Africa would also need to include policies that can promote the international competitiveness of the agro-food sectors. Under the two reform scenarios examined here, this region did not capture the potential benefits for private consumption that were suggested to be on offer if global reform efforts where more significant (Table 3.3). Given a "complete" reform scenario is highly unlikely, policies of the latter form would help the region better capture any potential benefits that may be on offer from reforms in their trading partners (for example when developed countries reform their policies).

The effects on consumption under the policy drift scenario show the costs of rising levels of distortions to agricultural markets. For most regions, the welfare effects proxied by consumption are negative. Importantly, these effects are largest in the countries that put in place higher levels of distortion to their agricultural markets – China, India, the Russia Federation and Malaysia along with Indonesia all experience losses. For the latter two, trade, total production and income all fall (along with agro-food exports).

Table 3.4. Impact of reform and drift scenarios on total production

% change

	Australia	New Zealand	China	Japan	Rest East Asia	Indonesia	Malaysia	Thailand	Rest South East Asia	India	Rest South Asia	Mexico	Canada	United States	Argentina	Brazil	Rest Latin America	European Union	Russia	South Africa	Middle East and North	Rest Sub Saharan Africa	Rest of the World
Policy drift																							
Total imports	-0.15	-0.08	-0.22	0.01	0.01	-0.35	-0.26	-0.01	0.00	-0.08	0.04	0.01	-0.02	-0.04	-0.08	-0.31	-0.02	0.00	-0.33	-0.01	0.02	-0.01	0.03
Total exports	-0.11	-0.03	-0.25	0.00	0.00	-0.29	-0.15	0.01	0.01	0.28	0.10	0.00	-0.01	-0.02	0.03	-0.16	-0.01	0.00	-0.26	0.00	0.00	-0.02	0.01
Total production	-0.02	-0.02	-0.06	0.00	0.01	-0.02	-0.08	0.00	0.00	0.20	0.02	0.00	0.00	0.00	0.02	0.00	0.00	0.00	0.02	0.00	0.00	0.00	0.01
Trade and domestic policy reform																							
Total imports	0.29	2.13	0.05	0.27	0.10	0.21	0.14	0.14	0.02	0.11	0.05	-0.01	0.19	0.05	0.58	0.77	0.14	0.09	0.19	0.09	0.07	0.05	0.15
Total exports	0.14	0.70	0.06	0.26	0.10	0.16	0.04	0.05	0.02	0.02	0.14	0.02	0.10	-0.01	-0.08	0.36	0.09	0.08	0.12	0.04	0.06	0.11	0.08
Total production	0.04	0.29	-0.01	0.02	0.06	0.00	0.04	0.03	0.00	-0.04	0.00	-0.01	0.00	0.00	0.04	0.04	0.02	0.01	-0.02	0.01	0.00	0.00	0.01
Policy reform all (developed and developing)																							
Total imports	0.74	3.50	0.32	0.14	0.37	0.99	0.46	0.45	0.23	0.18	0.37	0.02	0.37	0.19	0.97	1.63	0.43	0.08	0.58	0.29	0.25	0.33	0.41
Total exports	0.37	1.02	0.39	0.26	0.60	0.74	0.33	0.37	0.21	0.21	1.01	0.12	0.34	0.02	-0.14	0.70	0.46	0.07	0.67	0.19	0.38	0.65	0.49
Total production	0.10	0.51	0.02	0.01	0.41	0.05	0.22	0.14	0.02	-0.18	0.04	-0.02	-0.01	0.01	0.04	0.05	0.03	0.02	-0.07	0.04	-0.01	-0.01	0.00

Source: Author estimates from METRO.

Table 3.5. Impact of reform and drift scenarios on consumption

% change

	Australia	New Zealand	China	Japan	Rest East Asia	Indonesia	Malaysia	Thailand	Rest South East Asia	India	Rest South Asia	Mexico	Canada	United States	Argentina	Brazil	Rest Latin America	European Union	Russian Federation	South Africa	Middle East and North Africa	Rest Sub Saharan Africa	Rest of the World
												Policy drift											
Absorption	-0.01	-0.02	-0.01	0.00	0.01	-0.02	-0.11	-0.01	-0.01	-0.10	0.00	0.00	0.00	0.00	-0.02	-0.02	0.00	0.00	-0.03	0.00	0.01	0.00	0.01
Government consumption	0.00	-0.01	0.02	0.00	0.00	0.00	-0.04	-0.01	-0.02	-0.15	-0.02	0.00	0.00	0.00	-0.02	-0.01	0.00	0.00	0.02	0.00	0.00	0.00	0.01
Private consumption	-0.02	-0.03	-0.05	0.00	0.01	-0.03	-0.19	-0.02	-0.01	-0.15	0.00	0.00	0.00	-0.01	-0.03	-0.03	-0.01	0.00	-0.06	0.00	0.01	0.00	0.01
												Trade and domestic policy reform											
Absorption	0.03	0.43	0.00	0.01	0.01	0.02	0.10	0.08	0.01	0.03	-0.01	0.00	0.03	0.01	0.12	0.05	0.01	0.00	0.02	0.02	0.00	-0.02	0.03
Government consumption	0.00	0.21	0.00	0.00	-0.05	0.01	0.06	0.04	0.01	0.04	-0.01	0.02	0.02	0.01	0.06	0.03	0.00	-0.01	0.01	0.00	-0.02	-0.03	0.02
Private consumption	0.05	0.65	0.01	0.02	0.03	0.02	0.15	0.13	0.01	0.05	-0.01	-0.01	0.05	0.02	0.17	0.08	0.02	0.01	0.03	0.03	0.00	-0.02	0.05
												Policy reform all (developed and developing)											
Absorption	0.08	0.74	0.00	0.01	0.10	0.06	0.36	0.15	0.05	0.15	-0.02	-0.01	0.07	0.03	0.20	0.12	0.01	0.02	0.04	0.06	-0.03	-0.07	0.07
Government consumption	0.01	0.37	-0.02	0.00	-0.33	0.01	0.13	-0.03	-0.02	0.13	-0.11	0.06	0.01	0.02	0.10	0.08	-0.05	0.00	-0.03	-0.01	-0.13	-0.19	-0.01
Private consumption	0.14	1.09	0.02	0.01	0.26	0.11	0.59	0.26	0.08	0.23	-0.02	-0.02	0.12	0.05	0.28	0.17	0.03	0.04	0.08	0.10	0.00	-0.07	0.12

Source: Author estimates from METRO.

Notes

1. Developed countries to which the shocks are applied include Australia, New Zealand, Canada, the United States and the European Union 28. For some, as tariff levels 0 or close to the actual shock is small.
2. In China, MFN tariffs are close to bound rates but applied rates are more than 25% lower than bound making the increase feasible. That said, the increase in applied ad valorem equivalents modelled as tariffs can also depict changes in quota arrangements and other barriers that act in the same fashion as tariffs.
3. Food production includes processed rice, meat from cattle, sheep, goats and horse, other meat, dairy products, vegetable oils and fats, sugar and other food products.
4. In METRO, unlike e.g. the GTAP model, household and government are linked through the tax rates only and expenditures are independent from each other.
5. Investment is assumed to change proportionally with absorption and is therefore not affected by distributional issues.
6. For more details see Annex Figure 3.A2.3 and compare with Annex Figure 3.A2.5.

References

Anderson, K., J. Cockburn and W. Martin (2011), "Would Freeing up World Trade Reduce Poverty and Inequality? The Vexed Role of Agricultural Distortions", *The World Economy*, Vol. 34/4, Wiley, New Jersey, pp. 487-515.

Bouët, A. and D. Larborde (2009), "The Potential Cost of a Failed Doha Round", *IFPRI Discussion Paper*, No. 00886, IFPRI, Washington, DC.

Bouët, A., J-C. Bureau, Y. Becreux and S. Jean (2005), "Multilateral Agricultural Trade Liberalisation: The Contrasting Fortunes of Developing Countries in the Doha Round", *The World Economy,* Vol. 28/9, Wiley, New Jersey, pp. 1329-54.

de Melo, J. and S. Robinson (1989), "Product Differentiation and the Treatment of Foreign Trade in Computable General Equilibrium Models of Small Economies", *Journal of International Economics*, Vol. 27, Elsevier, Amsterdam, pp. 47-67.

Devarajan, S., J.D. Lewis and S. Robinson (1990), "Policy Lessons from Trade-Focused, Two-Sector Models", *Journal of Policy Modeling*, Vol. 12, Elsevier, Amsterdam, pp. 625-657.

Francois, J., H. van Meijl and F. van Tongeren (2005), "Gauging the WTO Negotiation's Potential Gains: Doha Round", *Economic Policy*, Vol. 20/42, Oxford University Press, Oxford, pp. 349-391.

McDonald, S., K.E. Thierfelder and T. Walmsley (2013), *Globe v2: A SAM Based Global CGE Model Using GTAP Data, Model Documentation*, available at: www.cgemod.org.uk/.

Narayanan, B.G., A. Aguiar and R. McDougall (eds.), (2012), *Global Trade, Assistance, and Production: The GTAP 8 Data Base*, Center for Global Trade Analysis, Purdue University.

OECD (2015), *METRO Version 1 Model Documentation,* OECD Publishing, Paris, www.oecd.org/officialdocuments/publicdisplaydocumentpdf/?cote=TAD/TC/WP(2014)24/FINAL&docLanguage=En).

OECD (2006), *Agricultural Policy and Trade Reform: Potential Effects at Global, National and Household Levels*, OECD Publishing, Paris, http://dx.doi.org/10.1787/9789264025745-en.

OECD-Food and Agriculture Organization of the United Nations (2015), *OECD-FAO Agricultural Outlook 2015*, OECD Publishing, Paris, http://dx.doi.org/10.1787/agr_outlook-2015-en.

Robinson, S., M.E. Burfisher, R. Hinojosa-Ojeda and K.E. Thierfelder (1993), "Agricultural Policies and Migration in a US-Mexico Free Trade Area: A Computable General Equilibrium Analysis", *Journal of Policy Modeling*, Vol. 15, Elsevier, Amsterdam, pp. 673-701.

Robinson, S., M. Kilkenny and K. Hanson (1990), *USDA/ERS Computable General Equilibrium Model of the United States*, Economic Research Services, USDA, Staff Report AGES 9049.

Tokarick, S. (2008), "Dispelling Some Misconceptions About Agricultural Trade Liberalization", *Journal of Economic Perspectives*, Vol. 22/1, AEA Publications, Pittsburgh, pp. 199-216.

Annex 3.A1

Regions, sectors and value added factors in the model

Table 3.A1.1. Regions in the study

No.	Code	Region	Comprising
1	aus	Australia	Australia
2	nzl	New Zealand	New Zealand
3	chn	China	China
4	rEAsia	Rest of East Asia	Hong Kong, Korea, Mongolia, Chinese Taipei, Rest of East Asia
5	jpn	Japan	Japan
6	rSEAsia	Rest of SE Asia	Cambodia, Lao PDR, the Philippines, Singapore, Viet Nam, Brunei Darussalam, Rest of South East Asia
7	idn	Indonesia	Indonesia
8	mys	Malaysia	Malaysia
9	tha	Thailand	Thailand
10	rAsia	Rest of South Asia	Bangladesh, Nepal, Pakistan, Sri Lanka, Rest of South Asia
11	ind	India	India
12	mex	Mexico	Mexico
13	can	Canada	Canada
14	usa	United States	United States
15	arg	Argentina	Argentina
16	rLAmerica	Rest of Latin America	Bolivia, Chile, Colombia, Ecuador, Paraguay, Peru, Uruguay, Venezuela, Rest of South America, Costa Rica, Guatemala, Honduras, Nicaragua, Panama, El Salvador, Rest of Central America, Dominican Republic, Jamaica, Puerto Rico, Trinidad and Tobago, Rest of Caribbean.
17	bra	Brazil	Brazil
18	eu28	European Union (28)	Austria, Belgium, Cyprus[a) b)], Czech Republic, Denmark, Estonia, Finland, France, Germany, Greece, Hungary, Ireland, Italy, Latvia, Lithuania, Luxembourg, Malta, Netherlands, Poland, Portugal, Slovakia, Slovenia, Spain, Sweden, United Kingdom, Bulgaria, Croatia, Romania.
19	rus	Russian Federation	Russian Federation
20	zaf	South Africa	South Africa
21	MENA	Middle East and North Africa	Bahrain, Islamic Republic of Iran, Israel, Jordan, Kuwait, Oman, Qatar, Saudi Arabia, Turkey, United Arab Emirates, Rest of Western Asia, Egypt, Morocco, Tunisia, Rest of North Africa.
22	sSSA	Rest of Sub-Saharan Africa	Benin, Burkina Faso, Cameroon, Cote d'Ivoire, Ghana, Guinea, Nigeria, Senegal, Togo, Rest of Western Africa, Central Africa, South Central Africa, Ethiopia, Kenya, Madagascar, Malawi, Mauritius, Mozambique, Rwanda, Tanzania, Uganda, Zambia, Zimbabwe, Rest of Eastern Africa, Botswana, Namibia, Rest of South African Customs.
23	row	Rest of World	Rest of Oceania, Rest of North America, Switzerland, Norway, Rest of EFTA, Albania, Belarus, Ukraine, Rest of Eastern Europe, Rest of Europe, Kazakhstan, Kyrgyztan, Rest of Former Soviet Union, Armenia, Azerbaijan, Georgia, Rest of the World.

a) *Note by Turkey*: The information in this document with reference to "Cyprus" relates to the southern part of the Island. There is no single authority representing both Turkish and Greek Cypriot people on the Island. Turkey recognises the Turkish Republic of Northern Cyprus (TRNC). Until a lasting and equitable solution is found within the context of United Nations, Turkey shall preserve its position concerning the "Cyprus" issue.

b) *Note by all the European Union Member States of the OECD and the European Union*: The Republic of Cyprus is recognised by all members of the United Nations with the exception of Turkey. The information in this document relates to the area under the effective control of the Government of the Republic of Cyprus.

Source: Authors' compilation.

Table 3.A1.2. Sectors in the study

No.	Code	Description	Comprising
1	apdr	Paddy rice	Paddy rice
2	awht	Wheat	Wheat
3	agro	Cereal grains nec	Cereal grains nec
4	av_f	Vegetables, fruit, nuts	Vegetables, fruit, nuts
5	aosd	Oil seeds	Oil seeds
6	ac_b	Sugar cane, sugar beet	Sugar cane, sugar beet
7	apfb	Plant-based fibres	Plant-based fibres
8	aocr	Crops nec	Crops nec
9	apcr	Processed rice	Processed rice
10	actl	Cattle, sheep, goats, horses	Cattle, sheep, goats, horses
11	aoap	Animal products nec	Animal products nec
12	armk	Raw milk	Raw milk
13	awol	Wool, silk-worm cocoons	Wool, silk-worm cocoons
14	acmt	Meat: cattle, sheep, goats, horse	Meat of cattle, sheep, goats, horse
15	aomt	Meat products nec	Meat products nec
16	avol	Vegetable oils and fats	Vegetable oils and fats
17	amil	Dairy products	Dairy products
18	asgr	Sugar	Sugar
19	aOfd	Processed Food	Food products nec, Beverages and tobacco products
20	Extraction	Mining and Extraction	Forestry, Fishing, Coal, Oil, Gas, Minerals nec.
21	TextWapp	Textiles and Clothing	Textiles, Wearing apparel
22	LightMnfc	Light Manufacturing	Leather products, Wood products, Paper products, publishing, Metal products, Motor vehicles and parts, Transport equipment nec, Manufactures nec.
23	HeavyMnfc	Heavy Manufacturing	Petroleum, coal products, Chemical, rubber, plastic prods, Mineral products nec, Ferrous metals, Metals nec, Electronic equipment, Machinery and equipment nec
24	Util_Cons	Utilities and Construction	Electricity, Gas manufacture, distribution, Water, Construction
25	TransComm	Transport and Communication	Trade, Transport nec, Sea transport, Air transport, Communication
26	OthServices	Other Services	Financial services nec, Insurance, Business services nec, Recreation and other services, Dwellings

Table 3.A1.3. Value added factors in the study

No.	Code	Description	Comprising
1	Land	Land	Land
2	tech_aspros	Technical	Includes ILO category Technical and Associate Professionals (major group 3)
3	clerks	Clerks	Includes ILO category Clerical Support Workers (major group 4)
4	service_shop	Service	Includes ILO category Services and Sales Workers (major group 5)
5	Off_mgr_pros	Professional	Includes ILO categories of Managers and Professionals (major groups 1 and 2
6	Ag_othlowsk	Ag & other	Includes Skilled Agricultural, Forestry and Fisheries Workers, Craft and Related Trades Workers, Plant and Machine Operators and Assemblers, and Elementary Occupations (major groups 6-9)
7	Capital	Capital	Capital
8	NatRes	Natural Resources	Natural Resources

Annex 3.A2.

Detailed results

Table 3.A2.1. Impact of removal of current policies: Contribution to production effects by region and sector

Regional share in total % change

	Australia	New Zealand	China	Japan	Rest East Asia	Indonesia	Malaysia	Thailand	Rest South East Asia	India	Rest South Asia	Mexico
Paddy rice	0.03	0.00	-0.08	-2.47	-0.06	-0.23	-0.09	0.58	0.03	-0.12	0.04	0.00
Wheat	-0.15	0.00	-0.36	-0.14	0.08	0.00	0.00	0.00	0.00	-0.77	-0.09	0.00
Cereal grains nec	-0.01	0.01	-0.15	-0.01	-0.04	-0.02	0.00	0.01	-0.01	0.01	0.00	-0.02
Vegetables fruit nuts	-0.01	0.00	0.05	0.07	0.03	-0.05	0.00	-0.04	0.04	0.07	-0.01	-0.06
Oil seeds	0.07	0.00	-2.09	-0.06	-0.20	0.87	0.73	-0.05	-0.01	-0.29	-0.01	0.00
Sugar cane sugar beet	0.16	0.00	-0.39	-0.10	0.07	-0.05	0.02	0.27	0.01	-0.92	-0.03	-0.12
Plant-based fibers	0.07	0.00	0.44	0.00	0.03	0.00	0.01	0.00	0.01	-1.07	0.47	0.04
Crops nec	-0.02	0.00	0.06	0.06	-0.09	-0.08	-0.28	-0.05	0.14	-1.13	-0.02	-0.08
Cattle sheep goats horses	0.36	0.27	-0.05	-0.22	-0.01	-0.01	0.00	-0.04	-0.05	-0.10	0.01	-0.11
Animal products nec	-0.01	-0.01	0.05	-0.39	0.19	-0.01	0.00	-0.02	-0.06	0.04	0.00	-0.03
Raw milk	0.04	0.23	0.05	-0.26	0.00	0.00	0.00	0.00	0.00	0.50	0.00	-0.02
Wool silk-worm cocoons	8.80	-0.40	-11.20	-0.01	0.08	0.00	0.00	-0.01	0.00	-0.24	0.02	0.00
Meat: Cattle sheep goats horse	0.38	0.32	-0.05	-0.40	-0.08	0.00	0.00	-0.04	-0.05	0.11	-0.01	-0.07
Meat products nec	-0.01	-0.02	-0.07	-0.61	0.13	0.00	0.01	-0.03	-0.07	0.01	-0.01	0.02
Vegetable oils and fats	-0.01	0.00	-1.44	-0.03	1.15	2.17	1.32	0.00	0.00	-0.73	-0.13	-0.03
Dairy products	0.07	0.15	0.04	-0.42	-0.03	0.00	0.02	0.00	0.02	-0.01	-0.05	-0.04
Processed rice	0.17	0.00	-0.07	-2.26	-0.09	-0.19	-0.20	0.72	0.11	-0.04	0.07	0.00
Sugar	0.07	0.00	-0.37	-0.28	0.24	-0.04	0.01	0.43	0.02	-0.49	-0.04	-0.15
Food products nec	0.03	0.00	-0.01	-0.02	0.45	-0.01	0.00	0.05	-0.01	-0.11	0.00	-0.01

Table 3.A2.1. Impact of removal of current policies: Contribution to production effects by region and sector (*cont.*)

Regional share in total % change

	Canada	United States	Argentina	Brazil	Rest Latin America	European Union	Russian Federation	South Africa	MidEast and North Africa	Rest Sub Saharan Africa	Rest of the World	World total
Paddy rice	0.00	0.63	0.00	-0.02	-0.09	-0.01	-0.05	0.00	-0.09	-0.06	-0.01	-2.08
Wheat	1.64	-1.39	0.04	0.01	0.04	0.43	0.67	0.02	-1.43	-0.02	0.62	-0.81
Cereal grains nec	-0.02	0.35	0.06	0.12	-0.02	0.25	-0.01	0.12	-0.10	-0.11	-0.02	0.38
Vegetables fruit nuts	0.06	0.11	0.01	0.00	0.03	0.03	-0.09	0.01	0.01	-0.07	-0.03	0.16
Oil seeds	-0.04	0.26	-0.50	0.71	0.26	0.33	-0.02	0.00	0.01	-0.01	-0.04	-0.06
Sugar cane sugar beet	0.00	-0.05	0.01	2.10	0.21	-0.32	-0.11	0.01	0.06	-0.18	0.00	0.67
Plant-based fibers	0.00	-1.43	-0.01	-0.06	0.05	-0.01	0.00	0.00	0.20	0.35	0.33	-0.58
Crops nec	-0.34	0.21	0.01	-0.11	0.05	0.54	0.00	0.00	0.08	0.26	-0.17	-0.97
Cattle sheep goats horses	0.00	0.24	0.48	0.17	0.38	-0.24	-0.06	-0.01	-0.55	0.08	-0.49	0.06
Animal products nec	-0.03	0.27	0.06	0.28	-0.03	0.30	-0.10	-0.01	-0.01	-0.03	-0.26	0.20
Raw milk	-0.61	0.15	0.04	-0.06	-0.04	0.74	-0.08	0.00	-0.15	-0.02	-0.14	0.35
Wool silk-worm cocoons	0.00	0.01	0.02	-0.02	0.11	0.89	-0.02	0.54	0.08	0.01	0.14	-1.19
Meat: cattle sheep goats horse	0.09	0.38	0.53	0.20	0.58	-0.91	-0.42	-0.01	-0.45	0.20	-0.68	-0.38
Meat products nec	-0.03	0.78	0.11	0.78	-0.04	0.84	-0.61	-0.02	-0.08	-0.08	-0.64	0.38
Vegetable oils and fats	0.01	0.06	-0.53	-0.19	-0.10	0.17	-0.06	0.01	0.16	-0.10	-0.09	1.60
Dairy products	-0.84	0.26	0.04	-0.03	-0.08	1.72	-0.10	0.00	-0.12	-0.03	-0.07	0.52
Processed rice	0.00	1.42	0.00	-0.02	0.03	-0.07	-0.07	0.00	-0.03	-0.06	0.00	-0.58
Sugar	-0.01	-0.10	0.01	1.80	0.36	-1.02	-0.35	0.10	0.18	-0.26	0.04	0.13
Food products nec	-0.01	0.12	0.01	0.04	0.02	0.40	-0.03	0.01	-0.07	-0.03	0.03	0.87

Table 3.A2.2. Impact of removal of current policies: Production effects by region and sector

% changes

	Australia	New Zealand	China	Japan	Rest East Asia	Indonesia	Malaysia	Thailand	Rest South East Asia	India	Rest South Asia	Mexico	Canada	United States	Argentine	Brazil	Rest Latin America	European Union	Russian Federation	South Africa	MidEast and North Africa	Rest Sub Saharan Africa	Rest of the World	World
Paddy rice	29.3	-0.7	-0.7	-32.9	-1.3	-2.6	-36.4	15.6	0.5	-1.5	0.8	-12.8	4.6	69.3	-2.5	-1.2	-3.2	-2.6	-20.1	-0.1	-2.7	-0.5	-2.2	-2.1
Wheat	-4.0	-1.8	-2.7	-73.5	47.8	-12.9	16.7	-51.5	10.6	-6.8	-2.1	1.1	46.7	-14.4	2.2	0.8	2.0	2.4	16.6	7.1	-8.9	-1.7	11.6	-0.8
Cereal grains nec	-1.3	9.2	-1.2	-18.1	-34.7	-1.0	1.9	3.8	-0.6	-0.2	0.3	-1.6	-1.3	1.5	2.3	2.5	-0.5	2.3	-0.8	17.3	-1.3	-0.3	-0.6	0.4
Vegetables fruit nuts	-1.2	-1.1	-0.4	2.4	2.2	-1.7	1.6	-2.9	1.8	0.6	-0.4	-4.0	11.3	1.6	1.7	-0.8	0.9	0.4	-3.2	1.1	0.4	-0.2	-1.0	0.1
Oil seeds	10.3	4.2	-17.4	-44.6	-76.0	16.9	11.2	-15.5	-1.0	-2.9	-0.2	4.7	-1.4	1.5	-7.1	5.8	9.3	4.0	-1.6	2.2	0.8	0.2	-2.3	-0.1
Sugar cane sugar beet	12.5	-0.2	-5.2	-15.1	35.4	-3.2	3.1	15.9	0.8	-6.3	-0.4	-4.5	0.4	-1.6	1.3	6.8	3.1	-5.4	-6.9	1.9	1.7	-4.2	0.0	0.6
Plant-based fibres	1.6	0.9	1.9	4.4	34.8	-2.0	7.1	0.6	4.0	-5.7	5.3	3.0	-0.4	-12.5	-1.4	-1.2	2.8	-0.5	0.1	0.6	1.8	5.8	8.3	-0.6
Crops nec	-2.2	-4.2	5.8	1.0	-6.6	-1.4	-55.9	-9.9	7.1	-6.4	-0.9	-6.1	-46.0	4.3	1.9	-0.9	0.6	2.5	-14.0	-0.9	5.7	3.4	-12.1	-1.0
Cattle sheep goats horses	11.7	22.9	-0.4	-12.8	0.1	-0.8	3.4	-17.9	-2.2	-2.3	0.8	-12.1	-0.1	1.6	17.6	1.9	9.3	-1.7	-3.7	-0.8	-9.2	1.9	-12.4	0.1
Animal products nec	-2.5	-10.6	-0.4	-17.1	8.3	-0.8	0.8	-2.2	-1.6	1.0	0.0	-2.0	-2.5	3.2	12.8	8.0	-0.4	2.2	-4.3	-1.3	0.0	-1.2	-11.8	0.0
Raw milk	3.5	8.8	-0.1	-11.0	0.7	-1.0	9.6	-1.6	0.4	2.0	0.2	-2.6	-36.7	1.2	3.4	-1.7	-0.7	3.5	-2.2	0.2	-1.3	-0.8	-3.2	0.3
Wool silk-worm cocoons	95.9	-35.3	-40.8	-0.6	4.8	-0.5	1.3	-3.4	-0.6	-2.3	5.3	-4.2	2.6	10.1	4.1	-0.2	7.7	64.0	-1.4	32.4	0.9	1.1	1.7	-1.3
Meat: cattle sheep goats horse	17.9	29.4	-1.7	-13.3	-3.8	-0.4	7.1	-18.3	-7.1	11.2	-0.5	-6.1	2.3	1.6	21.2	2.7	11.4	-6.3	-3.8	-0.5	-7.0	3.8	-22.1	-0.3
Meat products nec	-1.1	-9.7	-1.1	-22.4	6.5	0.1	7.9	-2.4	-2.9	1.9	-1.4	1.4	-1.7	4.8	18.1	16.5	-0.5	2.8	-30.5	-2.2	-1.9	-3.7	-33.8	0.3
Vegetable oils and fats	-2.0	0.7	-6.4	-2.0	126.4	27.7	13.1	0.7	-0.3	-11.5	-6.9	-3.6	0.2	0.9	-12.2	-2.5	-2.4	1.4	-3.1	2.1	5.3	-9.2	-4.8	1.5
Dairy products	4.8	10.5	-0.3	-13.4	-1.8	-0.5	9.6	0.4	5.6	-1.0	-1.0	-2.3	-41.5	2.1	3.6	-1.0	-2.1	4.5	-2.9	0.7	-1.7	-2.3	-1.3	0.5
Processed rice	39.2	-7.7	-1.2	-21.0	-2.7	-2.6	-35.4	17.3	1.4	-0.8	0.9	-0.9	-1.7	65.8	-0.8	-0.5	0.9	-3.5	-34.6	3.1	-1.1	-4.9	0.2	-0.6
Sugar	2.4	-8.9	-5.6	-13.0	36.0	-3.1	8.2	17.0	1.2	-5.0	-0.4	-4.9	-1.3	-1.5	1.8	10.9	4.9	-7.6	-7.5	8.4	3.2	-9.3	2.8	0.1
Food products nec	2.2	-0.3	-0.7	-0.3	24.3	-0.3	1.6	6.5	-0.2	-4.9	0.3	-0.8	-0.4	0.8	1.2	1.1	0.7	1.6	-1.5	1.8	-1.1	-0.8	1.3	0.8

Figure 3.A2.1. Impact of removal of current policies on export by use category

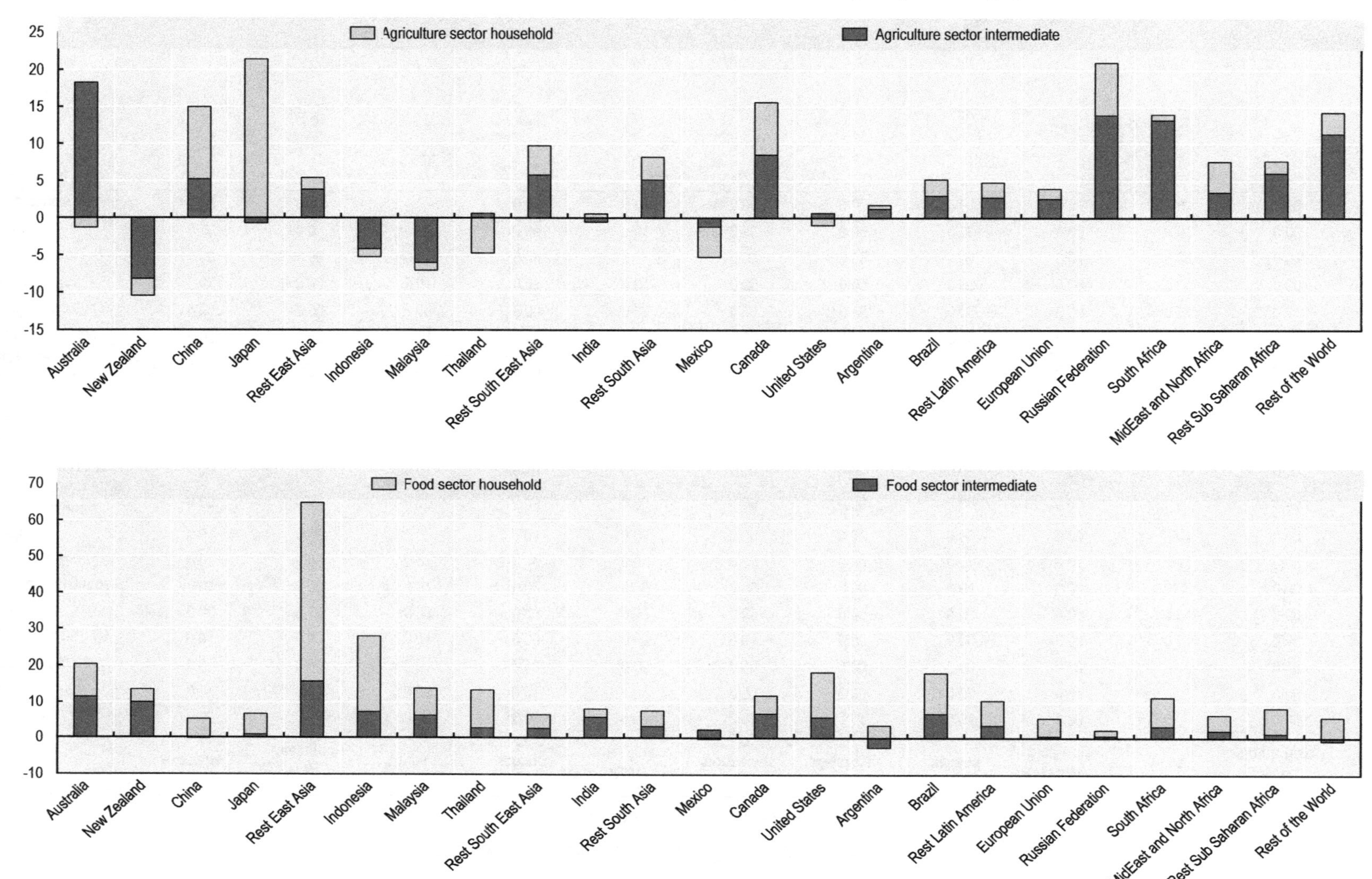

Table 3.A2.3. Scenario1: Effects of trade and domestic policy reform on production

Regional share in total % change

	Australia	New Zealand	China	Japan	Rest East Asia	Indonesia	Malaysia	Thailand	Rest South East Asia	India	Rest South Asia	Mexico
Paddy rice	0.00	0.00	-0.04	-0.08	-0.01	-0.02	-0.01	0.03	0.00	0.01	0.01	0.00
Wheat	0.07	0.00	-0.01	-0.05	0.01	0.00	0.00	0.00	0.00	0.02	0.00	-0.01
Cereal grains nec	0.00	0.00	-0.01	0.00	0.00	0.00	0.00	0.00	0.00	0.00	0.00	0.00
Vegetables fruit nuts	-0.01	0.00	0.01	0.00	0.00	-0.01	0.00	0.00	0.00	-0.01	0.00	-0.01
Oil seeds	0.00	0.00	-0.23	-0.02	-0.02	0.09	0.08	0.00	0.00	-0.01	0.00	0.00
Sugar cane sugar beet	0.01	0.00	-0.02	-0.02	0.00	0.00	0.00	0.04	0.00	0.02	0.00	-0.01
Plant-based fibers	0.01	0.00	0.22	0.00	0.01	0.00	0.00	0.00	0.01	0.14	0.08	0.02
Crops nec	-0.01	0.00	0.02	-0.01	0.00	0.00	-0.02	0.00	0.00	0.01	0.00	0.00
Cattle sheep goats horses	0.05	0.17	0.00	-0.06	0.00	0.00	0.00	0.00	0.00	0.01	0.00	-0.02
Animal products nec	-0.01	0.00	0.01	-0.10	0.01	0.00	0.00	0.00	0.00	0.00	0.00	0.00
Raw milk	0.00	-0.05	0.01	-0.05	0.00	0.00	0.00	0.00	0.00	0.00	0.00	0.00
Wool silk-worm cocoons	-0.01	0.00	0.00	0.00	0.00	0.00	0.00	0.00	0.00	0.00	0.00	0.00
Meat: cattle sheep goats horse	0.07	0.20	0.00	-0.10	0.00	0.00	0.00	0.00	0.00	0.02	0.00	-0.01
Meat products nec	0.00	0.00	-0.01	-0.15	0.01	0.00	0.00	0.01	0.00	0.00	0.00	0.01
Vegetable oils and fats	0.00	0.00	-0.18	0.00	0.05	0.20	0.15	0.00	0.00	-0.04	-0.01	-0.01
Dairy products	0.01	-0.03	0.01	-0.07	0.00	0.00	0.00	0.00	0.00	0.00	0.00	0.00
Processed rice	0.00	0.00	-0.01	-0.09	-0.01	-0.02	-0.02	0.04	0.01	0.02	0.01	0.00
Sugar	0.00	0.00	-0.02	-0.06	0.01	0.00	0.00	0.06	0.00	0.02	0.00	-0.01
Food products nec	0.00	0.00	0.02	-0.01	0.02	0.00	0.00	0.01	0.00	0.00	0.00	0.00

Table 3.A2.3 Scenario1: Effects of trade and domestic policy reform on production (*cont.*)

Regional share in total % change

	Canada	United States	Argentina	Brazil	Rest Latin America	European Union	Russian Federation	South Africa	MidEast and North Africa	Rest Sub-Saharan Africa	Rest of the World	World total
Paddy rice	0.00	0.01	0.00	0.00	-0.01	-0.02	0.00	0.00	-0.01	-0.01	0.00	-0.15
Wheat	0.31	-0.74	0.01	0.00	0.06	-0.04	0.16	0.01	-0.01	0.05	0.12	-0.04
Cereal grains nec	-0.01	-0.07	0.01	0.02	0.00	0.00	0.00	0.01	0.00	-0.01	0.00	-0.05
Vegetables fruit nuts	0.00	0.05	0.01	0.00	0.00	-0.02	-0.01	0.00	0.01	-0.01	0.00	0.02
Oil seeds	-0.02	-0.11	-0.12	0.06	0.02	0.06	0.00	0.00	0.02	0.00	0.00	-0.20
Sugar cane sugar beet	0.00	0.04	0.00	0.43	0.03	-0.14	-0.01	0.00	0.02	-0.03	0.01	0.36
Plant-based fibers	0.00	-0.93	0.00	0.07	0.04	0.01	0.00	0.00	0.12	0.10	0.05	-0.06
Crops nec	-0.21	0.06	0.00	-0.01	0.01	0.04	0.00	0.00	0.02	0.02	-0.02	-0.11
Cattle sheep goats horses	-0.03	0.03	0.11	0.07	0.07	-0.35	0.00	0.00	-0.04	0.00	-0.04	-0.02
Animal products nec	-0.05	0.09	0.00	0.06	0.00	-0.02	-0.01	0.00	0.00	0.00	-0.02	-0.04
Raw milk	-0.01	-0.05	0.00	-0.01	0.00	0.06	-0.01	0.00	-0.01	0.00	-0.01	-0.13
Wool silk-worm cocoons	0.00	0.00	0.00	-0.01	0.00	0.00	0.00	0.00	0.01	0.00	0.00	0.00
Meat: Cattle sheep goats horse	-0.04	0.04	0.12	0.07	0.13	-0.71	-0.02	0.00	-0.02	0.00	-0.03	-0.29
Meat products nec	-0.19	0.23	0.00	0.17	0.01	-0.09	-0.04	0.00	0.00	-0.01	-0.04	-0.10
Vegetable oils and fats	-0.01	-0.03	-0.11	-0.03	0.00	-0.02	0.00	0.00	0.07	-0.01	-0.01	-0.01
Dairy products	-0.01	-0.04	0.00	0.00	0.00	0.15	-0.01	0.00	-0.01	0.00	0.00	0.01
Processed rice	0.00	0.02	0.00	0.00	0.00	-0.04	-0.01	0.00	0.00	0.00	0.00	-0.12
Sugar	-0.02	0.05	0.00	0.36	0.06	-0.46	-0.03	0.01	0.07	-0.05	0.02	0.00
Food products nec	-0.01	0.02	0.00	0.01	0.00	0.02	0.00	0.00	0.00	0.00	0.01	0.10

Table 3.A2.4. Scenario2: Effects of policy reform all on trade

Regional share in total % change

	Australia	New Zealand	China	Japan	Rest East Asia	Indonesia	Malaysia	Thailand	Rest South East Asia	India	Rest South Asia	Mexico
Paddy rice	0.00	0.00	-0.19	-0.08	-0.06	-0.10	-0.04	0.10	0.02	-0.07	0.02	0.00
Wheat	-0.02	0.00	-0.14	-0.05	0.03	0.00	0.00	0.00	0.00	-0.34	-0.04	-0.01
Cereal grains nec	0.00	0.00	-0.07	0.00	-0.02	-0.01	0.00	0.01	0.00	0.00	0.00	-0.01
Vegetables fruit nuts	0.00	0.00	0.02	0.00	0.01	-0.02	0.00	-0.01	0.01	0.04	0.00	-0.03
Oil seeds	0.03	0.00	-1.40	-0.02	-0.09	0.33	0.32	-0.02	0.00	-0.12	-0.01	0.00
Sugar cane sugar beet	0.06	0.00	-0.16	-0.02	0.02	-0.02	0.00	0.11	-0.01	-0.43	-0.02	-0.04
Plant-based fibers	0.07	0.00	0.27	0.00	0.01	0.00	0.00	0.00	0.01	-0.57	0.23	0.02
Crops nec	-0.01	0.00	0.01	0.03	-0.03	-0.03	-0.11	-0.01	0.04	-0.51	-0.01	-0.04
Cattle sheep goats horses	0.12	0.14	-0.02	-0.05	0.00	0.00	0.00	-0.01	-0.02	-0.05	0.00	-0.07
Animal products nec	-0.01	0.00	0.12	-0.10	0.08	0.00	0.00	0.01	-0.02	0.02	0.00	-0.02
Raw milk	0.01	0.07	0.03	-0.05	-0.01	0.00	0.00	0.00	0.00	0.25	0.00	-0.01
Wool silk-worm cocoons	3.39	-0.24	-4.48	-0.01	0.06	0.00	0.00	0.00	0.00	-0.13	0.01	0.00
Meat: cattle sheep goats horse	0.13	0.16	-0.03	-0.09	-0.04	0.00	0.00	-0.01	-0.02	0.05	0.00	-0.05
Meat products nec	0.00	-0.01	0.04	-0.15	0.05	0.00	0.00	0.02	-0.03	0.00	0.00	-0.01
Vegetable oils and fats	0.00	0.00	-0.73	-0.02	0.35	0.84	0.59	0.01	0.00	-0.26	-0.06	-0.01
Dairy products	0.02	0.05	0.02	-0.07	-0.02	0.00	0.01	0.00	0.01	0.02	-0.02	-0.02
Processed rice	0.00	0.00	-0.06	-0.09	-0.06	-0.08	-0.10	0.12	0.05	-0.02	0.02	0.00
Sugar	0.02	0.00	-0.16	-0.06	0.08	-0.02	0.00	0.17	-0.01	-0.22	-0.02	-0.04
Food products nec	0.01	0.00	0.00	-0.01	0.16	0.00	0.00	0.03	0.00	-0.05	0.00	-0.01

Table 3A2.4. Scenario 2: Effects of policy reform all on trade (*cont.*)

Regional share in total % change

	Canada	United States	Argentina	Brazil	Rest Latin America	European Union	Russia	South Africa	MidEast and North Africa	Rest Sub-Saharan Africa	Rest of the World	World total
Paddy rice	0.00	0.06	0.00	-0.01	-0.04	-0.01	-0.02	0.00	-0.04	-0.03	-0.01	0.34
Wheat	0.58	-0.73	0.05	0.01	0.04	0.22	0.32	0.01	-0.63	0.00	0.19	0.48
Cereal grains nec	0.00	0.07	0.02	0.04	-0.01	0.09	-0.01	0.03	-0.05	-0.05	-0.02	-0.06
Vegetables fruit nuts	0.02	0.07	0.01	0.00	0.02	0.02	-0.04	0.00	0.01	-0.03	-0.01	-0.05
Oil seeds	-0.01	0.32	-0.15	0.32	0.07	0.15	-0.01	0.00	0.00	-0.01	-0.05	0.13
Sugar cane sugar beet	0.00	0.03	0.00	0.78	0.06	-0.12	-0.05	0.00	0.01	-0.08	0.00	0.24
Plant-based fibers	0.00	-0.83	0.00	0.00	0.03	0.00	0.00	0.00	0.11	0.17	0.16	0.25
Crops nec	-0.21	0.09	0.01	-0.05	0.06	0.22	0.00	0.00	0.02	0.13	-0.09	0.38
Cattle sheep goats horses	-0.01	0.10	0.13	0.04	0.10	-0.11	-0.03	0.00	-0.24	0.00	-0.20	0.17
Animal products nec	-0.04	0.13	0.01	0.09	-0.02	0.09	-0.05	0.00	-0.01	-0.01	-0.12	-0.18
Raw milk	-0.01	-0.04	0.01	-0.03	-0.03	0.19	-0.04	0.00	-0.08	-0.01	-0.10	-0.29
Wool silk-worm cocoons	0.00	0.00	0.01	-0.01	0.05	0.30	-0.01	0.19	0.03	0.00	0.07	0.62
Meat: cattle sheep goats horse	-0.01	0.13	0.15	0.05	0.16	-0.40	-0.20	0.00	-0.17	0.00	-0.22	0.13
Meat products nec	-0.11	0.35	0.01	0.27	-0.03	0.23	-0.27	-0.01	-0.04	-0.04	-0.28	-0.11
Vegetable oils and fats	0.00	0.05	-0.21	-0.08	-0.06	0.07	-0.03	0.00	0.04	-0.05	-0.09	-0.35
Dairy products	-0.01	-0.02	0.01	-0.01	-0.04	0.43	-0.05	0.00	-0.07	-0.02	-0.08	-0.13
Processed rice	0.00	0.03	0.00	-0.01	0.00	-0.03	-0.03	0.00	-0.02	-0.03	0.00	0.19
Sugar	-0.01	0.06	0.00	0.67	0.10	-0.39	-0.17	0.03	0.04	-0.12	0.01	0.04
Food products nec	0.00	0.05	0.00	0.01	0.01	0.17	-0.01	0.01	-0.03	-0.01	0.01	-0.24

Table 3.A2.5. Scenario3: Effects of policy drift on production

Regional share in total % change

	Australia	New Zealand	China	Japan	Rest East Asia	Indonesia	Malaysia	Thailand	Rest South East Asia	India	Rest South Asia	Mexico
Paddy rice	0.00	0.00	0.06	0.00	0.00	0.04	0.03	-0.02	-0.01	0.10	0.00	0.00
Wheat	0.02	0.00	0.05	0.00	0.00	0.00	0.00	0.00	0.00	0.34	-0.01	0.00
Cereal grains nec	0.00	0.00	0.03	0.00	0.00	0.00	0.00	0.00	0.00	0.01	0.00	0.00
Vegetables fruit nuts	0.00	0.00	-0.02	0.00	0.00	0.01	0.00	0.00	0.00	-0.05	0.00	0.00
Oil seeds	-0.01	0.00	1.35	0.00	-0.01	-0.10	-0.12	0.00	0.00	0.03	0.00	0.00
Sugar cane sugar beet	-0.02	0.00	0.06	0.00	0.00	0.01	0.00	-0.01	0.00	0.44	0.00	0.00
Plant-based fibers	-0.07	0.00	-0.18	0.00	0.00	0.00	0.00	0.00	0.00	0.74	-0.04	0.00
Crops nec	0.00	0.00	0.04	-0.01	-0.01	0.01	0.04	0.00	-0.02	0.49	-0.01	0.00
Cattle sheep goats horses	0.00	0.00	0.00	0.00	0.00	0.00	0.00	0.00	0.00	0.06	0.00	0.00
Animal products nec	0.00	0.00	-0.20	0.00	0.00	0.00	0.00	0.00	0.00	-0.01	0.00	0.00
Raw milk	0.00	-0.01	-0.03	0.00	0.00	0.00	0.00	0.00	0.00	-0.23	0.00	0.00
Wool silk-worm cocoons	-1.21	0.13	1.42	0.00	0.03	0.00	0.00	0.00	0.00	0.14	0.00	0.00
Meat: cattle sheep goats horse	0.00	0.00	0.01	0.00	0.00	0.00	0.00	0.00	0.00	0.00	0.00	0.00
Meat products nec	0.00	0.00	-0.11	0.00	0.00	0.00	0.00	0.00	0.00	0.00	0.00	0.00
Vegetable oils and fats	0.00	0.00	0.46	0.00	0.00	-0.27	-0.21	0.00	0.00	0.07	0.00	0.00
Dairy products	0.00	-0.01	-0.02	0.00	0.00	0.00	0.00	0.00	0.00	-0.01	0.00	0.00
Processed rice	0.00	0.00	0.02	0.00	0.00	0.03	0.07	-0.02	-0.02	0.09	-0.01	0.00
Sugar	0.00	0.00	0.06	0.00	-0.01	0.01	0.00	-0.02	0.00	0.23	0.00	0.00
Food products nec	0.00	0.00	0.01	0.00	0.00	0.00	0.00	0.00	0.00	0.04	0.00	0.00

Table 3.A2.5. Scenario 3: Effects of policy drift on production (*cont.*)

Regional share in total % change

	Canada	United States	Argentina	Brazil	Rest Latin America	European Union	Russia	South Africa	MidEast and North Africa	Rest Sub Saharan Africa	Rest of the World	World total
Paddy rice	0.00	0.00	0.00	0.00	0.00	0.00	0.01	0.00	0.00	0.00	0.00	0.21
Wheat	0.00	0.03	0.00	0.01	0.00	0.00	-0.06	0.00	0.00	0.00	0.00	0.36
Cereal grains nec	0.00	0.00	0.00	0.00	0.00	-0.01	0.00	0.00	0.00	0.00	0.00	0.04
Vegetables fruit nuts	-0.01	0.01	0.00	0.00	0.00	-0.01	0.01	0.00	0.00	0.01	0.00	-0.05
Oil seeds	-0.04	-0.38	-0.02	-0.30	-0.03	-0.02	0.00	0.00	-0.01	-0.01	0.03	0.37
Sugar cane sugar beet	0.00	0.00	0.00	-0.11	-0.01	0.00	0.02	0.00	-0.01	-0.01	0.00	0.35
Plant-based fibers	0.00	-0.10	0.00	0.00	0.00	0.00	0.00	0.00	-0.01	-0.03	-0.02	0.27
Crops nec	0.00	0.01	0.00	0.01	-0.02	-0.08	0.00	0.00	-0.02	-0.03	0.00	0.39
Cattle sheep goats horses	0.00	0.00	0.00	0.00	-0.01	-0.02	0.01	0.00	0.00	0.00	0.00	0.04
Animal products nec	0.00	0.00	0.00	0.00	0.00	-0.02	0.01	0.00	0.00	0.00	0.00	-0.21
Raw milk	0.00	0.01	0.00	0.00	0.00	-0.01	0.00	0.00	0.00	0.00	0.00	-0.28
Wool silk-worm cocoons	0.00	0.00	-0.01	0.00	-0.02	-0.06	0.00	-0.05	0.00	0.00	-0.01	0.36
Meat: cattle sheep goats horse	0.00	0.00	0.00	0.00	-0.01	-0.03	0.08	0.00	0.00	0.00	0.00	0.03
Meat products nec	-0.02	-0.01	0.00	0.01	0.00	-0.05	0.11	0.00	0.00	0.00	0.00	-0.08
Vegetable oils and fats	-0.01	-0.03	0.06	-0.02	0.00	0.00	0.01	0.00	0.01	0.00	0.09	0.16
Dairy products	0.00	0.00	0.00	0.00	0.00	-0.03	0.02	0.00	0.00	0.00	0.00	-0.05
Processed rice	0.00	0.00	0.00	0.00	0.00	0.00	0.01	0.00	0.00	0.00	0.00	0.18
Sugar	0.00	0.00	0.00	-0.09	-0.02	-0.02	0.07	0.00	-0.02	-0.01	0.01	0.17
Food products nec	0.00	0.00	0.00	0.00	0.00	-0.02	0.00	0.00	0.00	0.00	0.00	0.03

Annex 3.A3

Sensitivity of results to trade elasticities

METRO employs various trade elasticities that govern the response of the respective quantities to price changes. These are import and export elasticities on two different levels each. Depending on the elasticity level, a 1 percentage change of export prices has a lower or higher quantity effect. To test the sensitivity of model results to trade elasticities they were varied with the results compared to the basic setup. Figures 3.A3.1, 3.A3.2 and 3.A3.3 show effects on results with 15% lower elasticities and 40% higher elasticities on both the import and export side. The results are stable in respect to trade elasticities. Unsurprisingly, higher trade elasticities lead to stronger quantity effects and exports and imports increase stronger. In some regions, this leads to more positive effects in total consumption (absorption). However, besides the significant higher elasticities of 40%, the increases are moderate and relatively strong only in Japan. Lower elasticities on the other hand are decreasing the responsiveness to price changes, quantity effects are lower resulting in slightly lower changes.

**Figure 3.A3.1. Effects trade elasticity on absorption:
Lower elasticity -15%, base elasticity values and 40% higher elasticity**

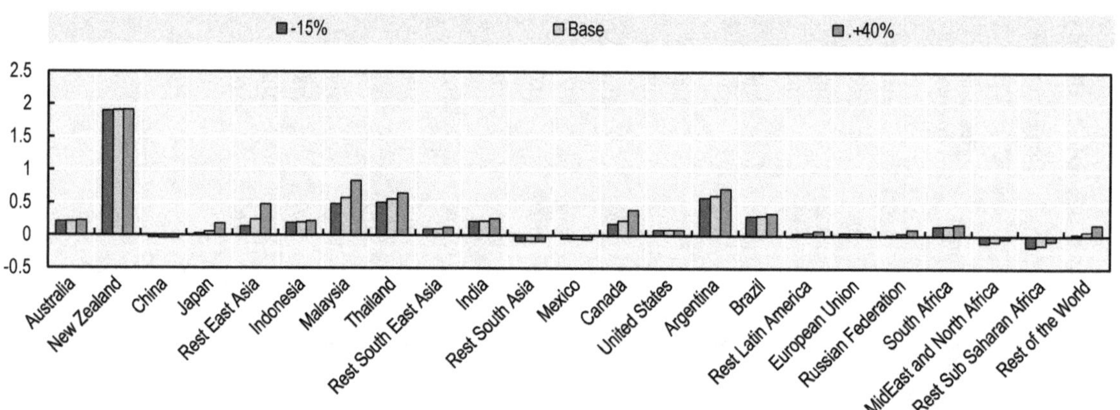

Figure 3.A3.2. Effects trade elasticity on imports: Lower elasticity -15%, base elasticity values and 40% higher elasticity

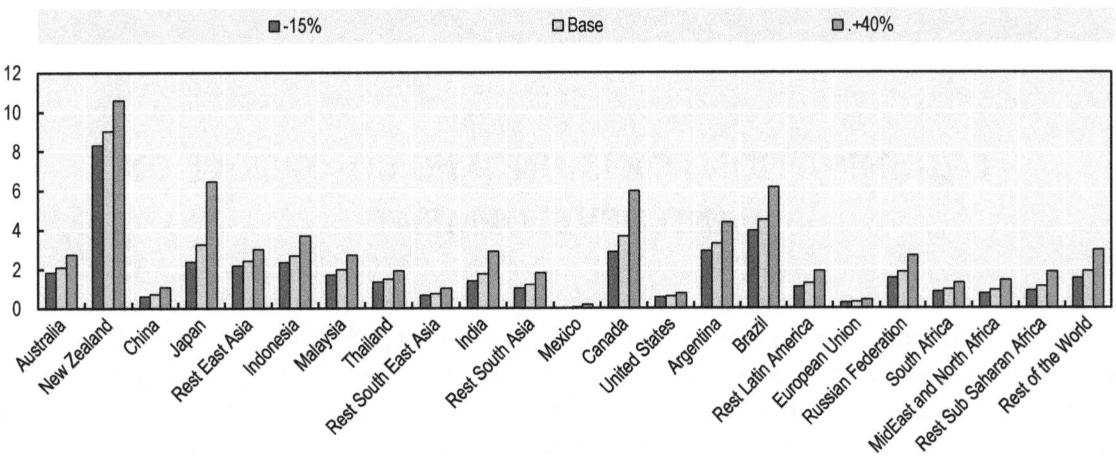

Figure 3.A3.3. Effects trade elasticity on exports: Lower elasticity -15%, base elasticity values and 40% higher elasticity

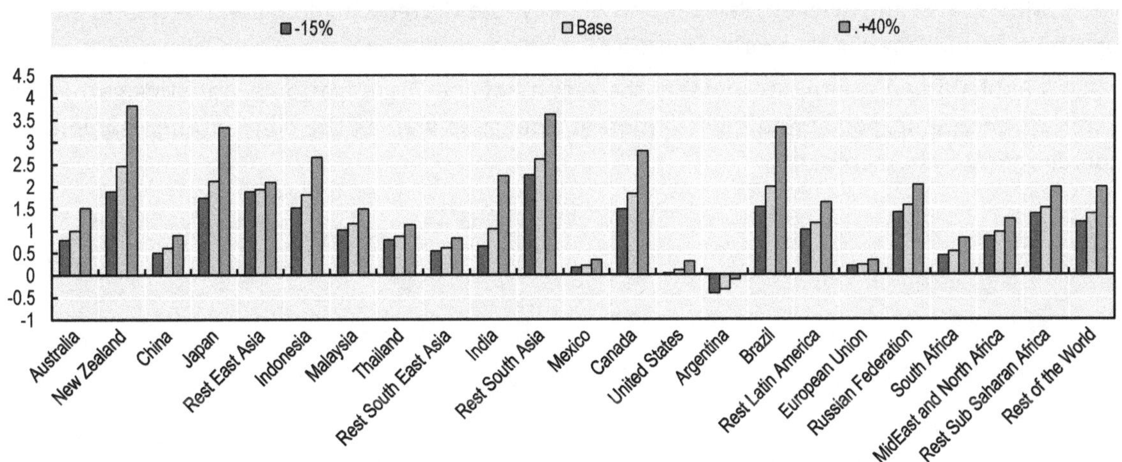

ORGANISATION FOR ECONOMIC CO-OPERATION AND DEVELOPMENT

The OECD is a unique forum where governments work together to address the economic, social and environmental challenges of globalisation. The OECD is also at the forefront of efforts to understand and to help governments respond to new developments and concerns, such as corporate governance, the information economy and the challenges of an ageing population. The Organisation provides a setting where governments can compare policy experiences, seek answers to common problems, identify good practice and work to co-ordinate domestic and international policies.

The OECD member countries are: Australia, Austria, Belgium, Canada, Chile, the Czech Republic, Denmark, Estonia, Finland, France, Germany, Greece, Hungary, Iceland, Ireland, Israel, Italy, Japan, Korea, Latvia, Luxembourg, Mexico, the Netherlands, New Zealand, Norway, Poland, Portugal, the Slovak Republic, Slovenia, Spain, Sweden, Switzerland, Turkey, the United Kingdom and the United States. The European Union takes part in the work of the OECD.

OECD Publishing disseminates widely the results of the Organisation's statistics gathering and research on economic, social and environmental issues, as well as the conventions, guidelines and standards agreed by its members.

OECD PUBLISHING, 2, rue André-Pascal, 75775 PARIS CEDEX 16
(51 2016 03 1 P) ISBN 978-92-64-26498-4 – 2016

www.ingramcontent.com/pod-product-compliance
Lightning Source LLC
LaVergne TN
LVHW081418110826
845149LV00010B/1788

* 9 7 8 9 2 6 4 2 6 4 9 8 4 *